Marie

Alf McCreary has written widely on Irish affairs, North and South, for a large number of publications in the British Isles, Europe and North America. Formerly Chief Feature-writer, and a Columnist and Leader-writer, with the *Belfast Telegraph*, he was the recipient of several British National Press and Regional Newspaper Awards for his work.

He is the author of a wide range of books, including three on victims of violence, namely *Survivors, Profiles of Hope* and *Tried by Fire*. Having travelled extensively around the world to carry out research for his books and articles, he lives and works in Northern Ireland, where he is Information Director at the Queen's University of Belfast.

Other titles by Alf McCreary

Corrymeela
Survivors
Up With People
Profiles of Hope
Spirit of the Age
Tried by Fire
An Ulster Journey
Remember When
Princes, Presidents & Punters

To the High Commissioner & Mrs. Eaton —

Marie

A story from
Enniskillen

Gordon Wilson
with Alf McCreary

With many thanks, & very best wishes.

Gordon Wilson.

COLLINS

MARSHALL PICKERING

Enniskillen.　　　　*10th April 92.*

William Collins & Co. Ltd
London · Glasgow · Sydney · Auckland
Toronto · Johannesburg

First published in Great Britain in 1990 by Marshall Pickering

Marshall Pickering is an imprint of
Collins Religious Division,
part of the Collins Publishing Group
8 Grafton Street, London W1X 3LA

Reprinted 1990

Printed and bound in Great Britain by
Billings & Sons Ltd, Worcester

Sales of this book will benefit the Royal Belfast Hospital for Sick Children Trust Fund,
and the Camphill Communities in Northern Ireland.

Contents

Acknowledgements

I would like to thank everyone who contributed to make this book possible. They include those who kindly gave permission for part of their sermons and letters to be included; to the BBC and its contributors for permission to use extracts from broadcasts; the *Belfast Telegraph* for the inclusion of its editorial comment; and those who assisted with the production, including Christine Whitell of Marshall Pickering, and Lorraine McCallum who helped with the manuscript. I pay special tribute to Joan Wilson and Hilary McCreary for their helpful comments and suggestions along the way.

Especially, I offer my grateful and heartfelt thanks to Alf McCreary, without whom the book could not, and indeed would not, have been written. His commitment was total. He gave generously of his mind and thoughts, of his professionalism and of himself. In our long journey together I came to know the quality of the man, and to appreciate the depth of his insights and his human touch. As a writer and a person he became a trusted friend and companion along the way.

Gordon Wilson

Enniskillen
2 April 1990

The Most Reverend Dr Robin Eames, Archbishop of Armagh and Primate of All Ireland

Armagh
June 1990

Many books and commentaries have been published on the tragic happenings in Northern Ireland. Words and comments, analysis and statistics, prophecies and advice, condemnation and claims, arguments and theories have filled book shops and provided the media with material in abundance. The world has grown used to the news of atrocities and apparently endless evidence of community division and alienation in this part of an island which was once renowned for its "saints and scholars". Behind the smokescreen of the violence, statistics and tension lives a community of ordinary, decent people, caught up in happenings and events over which they feel they have little or no control. Now and then the commentator and the theorist is reminded that those ordinary people do exist; that they lead lives with normal hopes and fears, joys and sorrows. Behind each statistic of terror, homes and families, men and women, young people and children carry the human burden of reaction, re-adjustment – and pain.

The tragic and horrifying events at Enniskillen on Sunday morning, 8th November 1987, will never be forgotten by those

of us who were there. Like so many other such events the world
learned of the details, registered its shock – and was prepared as
so often to move on to other things.

Quite suddenly a man called Gordon Wilson changed that
process.

His words, his attitude, his sheer human goodness and faith
shone out like a beacon of hope in the darkness. Faced with the
devastating loss of Marie his words of Christian understanding
were to become an inspiration to thousands. What he said and
did were of infinitely greater significance and meaning than the
bomb and the bullet.

Marie is one of the most moving and human stories to be
written from a situation of violence. In this book the personal
faith of a man cries out to be understood. His words are simple
and straightforward. They go to the heart of human suffering.
But they are a powerful and lasting testimony to the triumph
and faith of the human heart: for love and compassion are so
much stronger than hatred and bitterness.

It is my privilege to commend this book. I am quite certain
that *Marie* will find its place among the most important and
meaningful testimonies to the triumph of the human spirit.

+ Robert Armagh.

Day of Remembrance

On Sunday 8th November 1987, I was driving from Belfast to my mother's home in the small village of Bessbrook, set among the picturesque scenery of South Armagh near the Irish border. It was a grey morning, as befitting Remembrance Day, which has a special connotation in Northern Ireland. Groups of people were gathering around the Cenotaph in towns and villages to remember the dead of two World Wars, and of many conflicts since then – and not least in Northern Ireland itself.

The heroism of Ulstermen (and of Irishmen from Leinster, Munster and Connaught too) was legendary at the Battle of the Somme and elsewhere in World War One, and at Dunkirk and Arnhem, in Africa and the Far East and in many other places during World War Two. In Northern Ireland, thousands of homes are touched every Remembrance Sunday by deeply evocative memories.

On that particular Sunday I was remembering my grandfather, Thomas McCreary, who had fought at the Somme, and whose war medals have pride of place in my home, beside the German pipe which he brought back as 'war booty' and his blackthorn walking-stick. He rarely mentioned the War, but when he did he talked about the dirt and the slogging and the suffering and the bloodymindedness of it all. He had enlisted to take the place of his younger brother who, earlier, had talked his way past the recruiting sergeant, and had joined up, still under age. The younger brother was promptly sent home. My grandfather never glamourized war nor became sentimental about battle. He did what he felt he had to do, and he was glad to come home. His words and his memories gradually became part of my consciousness as I grew older and realized that there was a great deal to be said on both sides, and a great deal more than I had gleaned from my boyhood war films. Remembrance Sunday had become, to me, a day of sadness for the dead of all wars and conflicts, and also a moment for a personal renewal of a commitment to work where possible for the elimination of hatred and misunderstanding.

In my mind's eye I saw the usual group of people around the Cenotaph in my home village, with even fewer of the old soldiers like my grandfather who had passed on. Suddenly the background music on my car radio was punctuated by a news flash. A bomb had gone off at the Cenotaph in Enniskillen, as crowds gathered for the Remembrance Day services. First reports indicated serious casualties. Emergency and rescue services were rushing to the scene. It was scarcely believable, even to hardened veterans of hundreds of news flashes about violence in Northern Ireland. How could anyone place a bomb at a Cenotaph? It was like somebody mowing down a row of mourners at a funeral just because they were there. The dankness of that November day took on a darker dimension as more news filtered through. Pandemonium . . . people killed . . . heavy casualties . . . serious injuries.

My wife, who was beside me in the car, began to cry quietly, but I was now on the writer's 'auto-pilot', thinking about the magnitude of the story, how it would be covered, the ways in which the news services nationally and internationally on an otherwise quiet Sunday would be marshalled. There was another reason for my professional, and apparently detached, attitude. I had known a great deal about similar situations – or at that stage they had seemed similar – and I was thinking of the stories behind the big story. As a reporter and feature writer I had covered the aftermath of many bomb-blasts, and I had even written three books about the subject. I had talked to many victims of violence, and I knew what it was like once the cameras had moved on and the reporters had put away their microphones and notebooks. I had written about the pain of broken bodies and of the emptiness of homes where there were places missing at the family table. As my mind analysed the implications of each news flash from Enniskillen, I thought sadly of the victims and their families because my experience had made me aware of what they were going through, and what lay ahead.

For the rest of that day, the Enniskillen bomb and its implications failed to leave my mind. The purpose of our visit was to take part in a special birthday party for my mother, but even there, the news and the awareness of Enniskillen kept intruding. Later in the afternoon I took several of the younger children for a walk to the local pond where I had played as a boy. The darkness had almost closed in, and beyond their innocent shouts of glee as they fed the swans, my heart was heavy with the burden of sadness hanging over our unhappy land. As a boy I could remember better times when we played football and cricket and romped in these fields, far from the shadows of war. What had we come to, in God's name? The darkness closed in, and we walked back to the house with my question unanswered.

As we drove home, the reporters on the radio pieced together the story. Later, on television, the visual horror unfolded. Television has the power and professionalism to tell a horrific story extremely well. I remember the scenes of devastation, the rubble, the rescue workers, and the anguished face of the Anglican Archbishop of Armagh, Dr Robin Eames, who had been due to preach at the Enniskillen Remembrance Day Service, as he tried to find Christian words of comfort in front of the microphones and cameras, and tried also to explain the inexplicable. It was a Remembrance Day which no one would ever forget.

The next morning I listened to the radio, over breakfast. In Northern Ireland the local BBC Radio News carried further details, and then they broadcast an interview with a man called Gordon Wilson who had been caught directly in the blast with his daughter, Marie. She had been killed, and he had been injured. As he began talking I became absolutely frozen, with a cup of tea half-way to my lips. I could not move. His words, and his tone of barely controlled anguish, were burning deep into my very being:

> 'The wall collapsed . . . and we were thrown forward . . . rubble and stones . . . all around us and under us. I remember thinking. . . . "I'm not hurt" . . . but there's a pain in my shoulder. . . . I shouted to Marie, "Are you all right?" and she said, "Yes" . . . She found my hand and said, "Is that your hand, Dad?" . . . I said, "Are you all right, dear?" . . . but we were under six feet of rubble . . . three or four times I asked her . . . she always said, "Yes, I'm all right" . . . I asked her the fifth time . . . "Are you all right, Marie?" . . . She said, "Daddy, I love you very much. . . ." Those were the last words she spoke to me . . . I kept shouting, "Marie, are you all right?" . . . There was no reply . . . I have lost my daughter, but I bear no ill will, I bear no grudge. . . . Dirty sort of talk is not going to bring her back to life . . . I don't have an answer. . . . But I know there has to be a plan. If I didn't think that, I would commit suicide. . . . It's part of a greater plan, and God is good. . . . And we shall meet again.'

The news report went on to something else, but I still sat there transfixed. It was one of the most heart-rending, vivid and yet magnificent interviews I had ever heard, or will hear, in my lifetime. Gordon Wilson, in a few sentences, had said it all, for the bereaved, the injured, and the suffering, and for the rest of us who were suffering with and through him. Around the world, over the next few days, millions were to catch a glimpse and to share in that anguish of a soul at the extremity of heartache and loss and yet to share the love, and to note, incredulously, the total lack of ill-will. Gordon Wilson and Enniskillen and Remembrance Sunday had become part of the collective and individual experience of all of us who had ears to hear or eyes to see. His words, at that moment, conveyed more than the power of speech.

During the rest of that day I worked in my office, and that evening I left by boat to travel to Liverpool and then to London and Northern France where I was due to visit the Somme battlefield on Armistice Day, 11th November. And on that day, in the sombre silence of the battlefield, the carnage of Enniskillen came back into my mind, not from a distance but from the very spot on which I stood. The suffering of Enniskillen and of the Somme were one.

In subsequent days I travelled to other battlefields, including Vimy Ridge and the impressive Canadian War Memorial. By the time I returned to Northern Ireland the Enniskillen funerals were over, and the atrocity had dropped out of the main headlines. However, it was difficult, during the next few weeks and months, not to notice Gordon Wilson as he graciously collected awards which had been showered on him in memory of his daughter and in appreciation of his noble words. He seemed a man of dignity and of integrity. And he appeared to have the sense not to allow himself to be propelled forward by events to form a new peace movement. Others had done so in the past, and their dreams had turned to ashes. Gordon Wilson wisely slipped out of the headlines.

About twelve months later, I had a phone-call from Christine Whitell, Publishing Manager of Marshall Pickering, with whom I had worked on a previous book about the victims of violence, and she asked whether I might like to consider helping to write Gordon Wilson's story. I expressed an interest, but told her that he might not want to break his self-imposed silence. Nothing happened, but just over a year later she rang back to say that Gordon was indeed interested and that he would be glad if I could help.

A few weeks afterwards we had dinner at an hotel half-way between Belfast and Enniskillen, and I met this tall, pleasant man with the firm handshake, the friendly smile and the no-nonsense manner. We talked at length and, with an openness which I have come to know well, he explained his reasons for trying to produce a book and his fears about doing so. He was not keen on stirring up publicity again, and he did not want to be regarded as the only one who had suffered in Enniskillen. But he had three powerful reasons for wishing to put his experiences on paper — to produce some kind of written memorial for Marie, whose voice had been stilled by the bomb; to share his experiences in the hope that they might bring encouragement and comfort to others; and as a therapy for himself by talking through some of his deepest and perhaps unspoken feelings. We thought it over, and decided to meet again. I respected Gordon for his directness, and after some further consideration we eventually agreed to work together.

Over the next year I got to know Gordon Wilson as a man of integrity and of deep humanity. I also came to know Joan, Marie's mother, whose depth of insight and power of expression are most impressive. Together, as individually, they are remarkable people. I also came to know Marie's brother Peter and sister Julie Anne and they, too, have been touched by the fires, and are courteous, yet strong. They have all taught me something about dignity and humanity, in that magnificently matter-of-fact way in which so many Ulster families face the tragedies they are forced to bear. And they all taught me something deeper about the power of love.

At the start of my journey with Gordon Wilson, for that's what it has been, I hoped privately that the man whom I had so respected from afar would not have feet of clay. So often, in a writer's life, that can happen. But Gordon Wilson did not disappoint me. To borrow an accolade he so carefully bestows on only a few people, Gordon Wilson is 'a very sound man'. Our journey together has been sometimes almost unbearably moving, occasionally with a hint of humour, inspiring and unforgettable. It has been one of the great privileges of my life as a writer to be allowed to accompany Gordon Wilson on that journey. As a reader I hope and know that you will feel the same.

Alf McCreary

Belfast
St Patrick's Day, 17th March 1990

Christian compassion saved a bloodbath of revenge killings from angry loyalists.

Daily Mirror, 1st May 1989

. . . words of love after the atrocity stunned millions.

Belfast's *News Letter*, 8th June 1988

This inspiring man lacks bitterness, praying nightly for those who, under cover of darkness, planted the bomb.

Sunday Independent, 30th October 1988

From time to time we . . . see some inspiring examples of tolerance. Mr Gordon Wilson . . . impressed the whole world by the depth of his forgiveness.

His strength, and that of his wife, and the courage of their daughter, came from their Christian conviction.

H.M. The Queen, Christmas Day Message, 1987

To watch Gordon Wilson at his daughter's graveside was to witness a man with a shattered heart and a faith stronger than iron.

Daily Mirror, 11th November 1987

The words of Gordon Wilson as he described his personal tragedy moved the hearts of people throughout the world.

Tom King, then Secretary of State for
Northern Ireland, at the presentation of
the first "Marie Wilson Voyage of Hope" awards

Mr Wilson, for one, has generated much hope that good may yet come from Marie's brutal and untimely death.

Sunday Times, 15th November 1987

Gordon Wilson . . . one bright light shining across the globe . . . a man of unshakeable faith.

Enniskillen's *Impartial Reporter*, 12th November 1987

...within hours of last year's bomb, reprisals were planned ... it was because of the heroic spirit of forgiveness voiced by Gordon Wilson ... that the situation was defused.

Sunday Mail, 23rd October 1988

Gordon and Joan Wilson can't find it in their hearts or their faith to hate anyone, even the bombers who brought horror to Remembrance Sunday in Enniskillen.

Scottish *Catholic Observer*, 5th May 1989

Gordon Wilson ... has shown ... how indomitable the human spirit is. How decent men and women will neither be cowed into submission by terrorists nor coerced into copying them.

The war, the total war, against the IRA will be long and hard. But while there are men like Gordon Wilson it will be won.

Daily Mirror, 10th November 1987

CHAPTER ONE

The Wilsons

So much has happened to us during the past two or three years that it is extremely difficult to know where to begin. The Enniskillen bomb tore apart our family and the families of so many others. Eleven people died, and many people were injured, some of them dreadfully so. The bomb made national and international headlines, and there was sympathy and revulsion from people all around the world. Enniskillen was one of the most widely reported atrocities of the entire "Troubles" in Northern Ireland, and the fact that the bomb went off near the town's main Cenotaph on Remembrance Sunday will not be forgotten quickly or easily.

In personal terms I was pitch-forked from the obscurity of being a draper in Enniskillen to the international news headlines mainly through one interview on the evening of the explosion. It was a role which I did not seek and for which I was ill prepared. This in turn led to more publicity surrounding the awards given to me either directly or in memory of our daughter Marie. Over the months and years which followed, the name of Enniskillen remained associated with the Remembrance Day bombing, and the wide sympathy for the town and its people is still evident. And, on a positive note, there have been a number of developments in Enniskillen and elsewhere which give me hope for greater understanding and forbearance in the wake of such a terrible tragedy.

Yet at the heart of all of this was our devastating personal

loss of Marie in circumstances which we will never forget. The
central person in this story is Marie Wilson, and the best place
to begin is with Marie herself.

She was born into what I would like to think is an ordinary
family. She was the youngest of three. Her brother, Peter, was
eleven years older, and she was seven years younger than her
sister Julie Anne. A little boy was born prematurely shortly after
Peter, but we lost him.

I suppose that the youngest child is always that bit special.
Marie grew up as a normal little girl, sometimes strong-willed
and on occasions precocious, but full of charm. She was no
saint, and I would not want to make out that she was. But
she had enormously lovable qualities. She was, I suppose, the
"apple of my eye", though when I say that, it is no reflection
on Peter or Julie Anne, both of whom I love dearly. We are
a very close-knit family. It is hard to believe, after so many
days and weeks, and now years, of shock, suffering and loss,
that Marie has gone. Somehow, her presence still permeates the
house. There are some days when you still expect her to fling
open the back door, to burst into the room and exclaim, 'I'm
back again! I'm here! What's for tea?' But she isn't here, and
my wife Joan and I have tea on our own. The others are grown
up. They still come round regularly, and we keep in touch every
day. Joan and I are alone together in the family house now, with
our own company. Maybe that's the way it is in any family, with
the young ones growing up and finding their own path in life.

Marie, in a way, is still part of that family, part of our
memories and part of the past, yet strangely she remains a part
of our present. You can't destroy a memory by a bomb-blast.
In a real sense, Marie remains a part of our collective past and
present in a family that was typical until the bomb changed
everything.

When I say that our family was typical, I am looking back with
Joan and remembering falling for each other, getting married
and having children, just like other people all over the world.
But, in one sense, no family is typical. Each is a special unit, with
individuals blending as a whole, with their ups and downs, and
their good days and their bad days. So, to begin to understand

Marie and her background, and to get to know her as part of our family, it is necessary perhaps to go back a great deal further and to begin by looking at the elements which shaped the Wilsons, and not only her parents and brother and sister but also her grandparents as well. Without doubt, we are all part of the particular forces which have helped to mould Ireland and its people and its history, for better or for worse.

The Wilson family has been in Enniskillen since 1946, but our roots go deeper into the soil around a place called Manorhamilton, which is just across the border from Northern Ireland, in County Leitrim. I daresay that the Wilson stock could be traced to some of the Scots settlers, who came to the North of Ireland during the Plantation of the seventeenth century. But I haven't had the time, or indeed the inclination, to go back that far. It is sufficient to note that I was born in the Irish Republic, in Manorhamilton, and that my father was a small-town draper there. Times were hard. My father was one of a family of six who were reared in a three-roomed thatched cottage at the bottom of Benbow Mountain, some three miles outside Manorhamilton. They were small farmers, and quite poor. Every penny counted, and some of the family had to emigrate to Canada or New Zealand to make a decent living.

At the age of fifteen and a half, my father began his apprenticeship as a draper. He was born in 1897, so I'm talking about his early life not long before the outbreak of the First World War. During the War he stayed in the drapery business, and in 1925 he bought a shop in Manorhamilton. A year later he married my mother, a Miss Henrietta Conn, from Ballykelly in Co. Londonderry. She had trained in the Royal Victoria Hospital as a nurse, and maybe Marie, who also trained as a nurse in 'The Royal', had more than a fair share of her grandmother's blood in her veins!

My mother, who was called "Etta", decided to take up Home Nursing in Manorhamilton, and that's how she met my father. She had come to nurse an elderly man in one of the bigger houses locally and was "live in nurse". I would like to think that they met in a local church. Oddly enough my parents never told us how they met. Such things were not discussed in those days.

However, we know that they were married in my mother's home near Ballykelly, where my grandfather was a farmer. My parents spent their honeymoon in Killarney, and there's a family picture of my father and mother on horseback. They settled down in Manorhamilton, a young man making his way in the drapery business, and my mother with the home-making skills and the touch of a nurse. Eventually they had a family of four – three girls and me. I was born, the eldest, in 1927. My eldest sister, Joan, married Hedley Plunkett, a Fermanagh man who became a Methodist minister. My second sister, Wilma, married Harry Darling, a Kent man who was the local Surveyor of Customs, and she worked in the family business until quite recently, and my youngest sister, Dorothy, lives in Enniskillen. We were a happy family, but money was by no means plentiful. My father once told me that when I was born he took out an insurance policy for me, but that money was so short he had to take out a 'waiver' for one year because he could not afford the annual premium of £28! With such a background you learned to value things, but also that there was more to life than money. My father was a great fisherman, and he was in the right part of the world for enjoying his favourite pastime. The salmon and trout fishing around Sligo, Leitrim and Fermanagh is among the best in the world.

My father was so good at his hobby that he fished for Ireland, despite the pressures of his business, and one of my abiding images of him is with a rod and net, completely relaxed. He was the sort of man who believed that if a thing is worth doing, it is worth doing right! So it was no surprise that he ended up as a fisherman of international stature. He fished for Ireland five or six times in international trout fly-fishing competitions between the Home Countries at Loch Leven in Scotland, just north of a line from Glasgow to Edinburgh. He was a man of many achievements, and not the least of these was the establishment, with the help of others, of two small factories in Manorhamilton. One produced buttons and the other knitwear. At best they would have employed a total of thirty people, and that was quite something in such a small town in those days. He was also a fervent Methodist, and we went to the local church every Sunday. It is hard to judge just how that helped to shape us as children; but certainly I have been an active Methodist all my life. My father once told me that around the turn of the century there were more than a hundred children at the Methodist Church's Sunday School in Manorhamilton, but by the time I left those numbers had dropped dramatically. It was one indication of the dwindling numbers of Protestants in the Irish Republic, and that, of course, had significant implications for the future.

Part of my character was shaped in the local primary school and later at Wesley College, a well-known and highly-regarded boarding school in Dublin. This, as the name implies, had and still has strong connections with Methodism. Three days after the outbreak of the Second World War, in 1939, I began as a boarder at Wesley. Two months later my father took the lease on a shop in Enniskillen, and the Wilsons were destined to move into Northern Ireland. At the end of my first term in Wesley, and during the Christmas holidays, my father offered me the choice of staying on at Wesley College, or going to Portora Royal School, which had a long and distinguished history and which boasted such famous Old Boys as the hymn-writer Henry Francis Lyte, and playwrights Oscar Wilde and Samuel Beckett. However, I chose to stay at Wesley College. It seemed to me to be "Big Time", with more than five hundred boys and girls, and I liked being in the city. So I might say that 'My War' was spent near St Stephen's Green in Dublin, beside the Methodist Centenary Church! One night the German Air Force dropped bombs over Dublin, and that was the first time in my life I heard a bomb going off.

The time came, however, to move on. The Principal of Wesley College, the late Dr Irwin, retired the same day that I left Wesley. Maybe he had had enough when he had seen Wilson through! However he wrote me a letter which I have, to this day. It read as follows: "Dear Wilson, I enclose your results and Leaving Certificate. I suppose that you will be going into the family business. If not, will you consider medicine?" It was an important letter to me, and the nearest I ever got to careers advice. The School Careers Service was not a force in the land in 1945! I knew that my father all but expected me to go into the family business. I was the only son, and those were the days when sons were expected to succeed fathers. But I was not terribly sure about what I wanted to do. I used to help out in the shop in Manorhamilton on Fair Days, when every transaction developed into a "haggle", apart from the important business of getting a man what he wanted and what actually fitted him, which were not always one and the same thing. So you might start with the marked price of, say 2/11d for a cap. He would offer two shillings, and you might settle for 2/6d. I was never too sure, at that stage, whether or not I had enough 'bottle' for that kind of world.

At the end of June 1945, I was at a crossroads. There was a "Fair Day" on 1st July, and my father assumed that I would come in to help. I said to myself, 'This is decision time. This is the day to go in and to really sort yourself out, and decide whether or not you want to make a living out of this business.' So, I went in, full of heart, and determined to test myself. By the time the shop had closed I was satisfied that this was indeed the life for me. I felt that I could cope, and in my youthful ignorance I felt that I had had enough formal education. My parents asked me anxiously if I really wanted to try medicine, and, if so, they would do their best to support me. But I said, "No thanks". I'd had enough of exams and I was ready to make my way in the world. On 1st September 1945 I started my life's work, as a trainee in the Enniskillen store, while my father ran the shop which he had retained in Manorhamilton. But before I could conquer the world, there were a great many rough edges that needed to be knocked off.

There were other things which I had to learn about too, and they took some learning. I was shocked about what I found in the North, in terms of religion and politics. Very quickly I realized that life across the border was not as I had imagined it. In Manorhamilton the Protestants were in a minority compared to the Roman Catholic population, but in the Enniskillen area they were in roughly equal proportions. My mother was a Northerner, and maybe one of her unspoken or subconscious motives in coming to live in the North from the Republic was to find the right kind of husbands for her daughters. The thought would hardly even have occurred to my father. The way of the world proved to be very different in the North, and with my limited experience of life, it took a long time for those changes to register. In Fermanagh many jobs and houses were allocated according to political belief or religious persuasion on both sides, rather than on the primary considerations of ability or need. In Manorhamilton I had not been aware of this, but around the age of eighteen when I came North I found it to be a whole new ball game. Working in a shop which served the entire community I soon had to learn how people were thinking and behaving, on both sides of the house. But although I could understand what they were thinking, and maybe even why, I did not always agree with them. During my formative years in Manorhamilton and Dublin I had never felt any difficulty as part of the Protestant minority. I knew that there were divisions up North, but I did not realize how strongly-felt and firmly-held their differing opinions were. I was shocked, for example, by the harsh and biased words of some local government representatives as reported in the weekly newspapers. It seemed to me that neither side pulled their punches.

Some attitudes surprised me, and in certain cases they shook me. So during all these years in Enniskillen, and my working life has lasted for nearly forty-four years, I have never become involved in the party political scene. Perhaps I was always scared. I am the sort of man who does not take a hard line or hold strong views. I have always had my own thoughts and my own judgements, right or wrong, and I have tried to be fair. Not getting involved gave some immunity, but all the while, close to the surface, was the conviction that a lack of tolerance existed on both sides. People tended to live and work and be educated among their own folk. To my simple mind it did not make a difference whether a man was a Protestant or a Roman Catholic; I respected a person's point of view and I stayed away from conversations about religion or politics. I don't want to sound pious or other-worldly, it was simply that I felt it was safer to keep away from such contentious issues. I was happy to try to be a friend to all, and an encmy of none.

But this was the Enniskillen of forty years ago. People were born into one or other community, they accepted a certain point of view, so the same fixed attitudes and loyalties went on and on, from generation to generation. I always tried to see the man or the woman rather than the religious or political label, and I realized that whatever was beneath, the labels were only superficial. The Protestant-Roman Catholic thing was much more deep-rooted than I had ever imagined it would or could be. Perhaps it was fear or a lack of guts on my part not to confront this, but I wanted to be friends with everyone as far as I possibly could. Rather than sounding off, I tried by my actions and words to make friends, and I did so, on both sides.

Of course there were other kindred souls. I was not the only one who refused to take sides, but I soon realized that the potential for being misunderstood by both sides was great. Some Protestants might have seen me as a 'blow-in' from the Republic, and some Roman Catholics might have suspected me because I was a Protestant, and might have assumed that I would automatically take a "Protestant" line. I was never a "crusader", but simply tried to be my own man. I would like to have been regarded as a "moderate". Some might have said, "He's wishy-washy", but I could live with that.

It's important, however, to keep the record straight on such things. The vast majority of people on both sides were, and are, decent folk. There was a great deal of 'come and go' between the people of Enniskillen, and there still is a lot of common, honest-to-God decency across the board. But as a young man making my way in life within that community there was often an undercurrent which would come out in something that was said or done, on both sides, and which was really unworthy of us, but it was still there. On a number of occasions there were brick walls which I had to face on my journey, where one had to say "Yes" or "No" to a certain situation, and hope that one had the grace to do what seemed to me to be the right thing, and go on living with one's conscience.

There were serious political matters, but they also had sometimes almost comical overtones, if they had not been so sad. In our Draper's Shop we stocked men's lambswool underwear. It was thick-knit, very warm, and just right for farmers. Originally we bought it from a Yorkshire manufacturer and their label featured a Union Jack. Believe it or not there were Roman Catholic customers of ours, decent people, who refused to buy it because of the label. They saw it as British flag-waving. Some years later that particular brand was no longer made by that Yorkshire firm and we found a supplier of similar-type knitwear in Dublin. Their label stated "Made in the Republic of Ireland", and some of my Protestant customers refused to buy it. Perhaps only people in Ireland could understand that!

Sometimes in conversation with a friend I would feel that I was being two-faced, in order not to create an argument or to displease someone. I would decline to make a comment or give an opinion for the sake of not starting a row or something like that. And yet I tried as best I could to make a point of showing that I did not agree with what was being said or with the general drift of conversation about "so and so". People might say things like, "He's one of them", and the implication was "Watch him". And the man talking to you might have thought that you were agreeing with him. It was not easy to be direct and say, "Well, I don't agree with you", but I did take that approach when I felt it was necessary. But life went on from day to day, and one never really sat down and thought it through seriously, or tried to figure out all the answers. One got on with taking the children to school, and with bringing home the bread and butter, or getting the car fixed or one of the many ordinary things of life.

Often one felt sorry about the way things were, especially as so many people were decent in so many other ways. There was an attitude of sometimes talking scathingly about "the other side", and whatever the conversation you could very easily, and even unwittingly, touch a raw nerve that could hurt, or antagonize either side. One could get in trouble verbally without even trying. Religion and politics were always difficult, tricky subjects. I sometimes felt that I was accepted because I was a Protestant first, and not necessarily because I was "Gordon

Wilson" . To some people, that kind of thing seemed to matter. That was the way they behaved. Some would say, "Many of my best friends are Catholic, or Protestant", but others could not bring themselves to go that far, or even to mix with the "other side of the house". I remember a friend going with me to the funeral of a Roman Catholic neighbour. On the way into the chapel my friend said, "I'd rather not go any further. I'll just stay outside." That was his way of paying his respects. He could go only so far, then something stopped him. I suppose people were tribal, to a greater extent than I had imagined or wanted to believe. Maybe this is difficult for people outside Northern Ireland to understand.

To a certain degree life was a tightrope, but you got on with what you were doing. I could sell a man a suit without worrying or even thinking about his religious or political views. And there were a whole lot of other people who held moderate views and who wanted to get on with their lives, but for each there was a point at which they tended to retreat up their own cul-de-sacs. There are very few people in Enniskillen today but that I would not know how far their tolerance would stretch. I often wonder how far mine would stand scrutiny.

I would hate to give the impression that Gordon Wilson thought that he was better than anyone else, because that is not so, but I did not feel I belonged to any tribe, I had my own views, and that was that. I'm still not a member of any tribe; I am as I am. Things have improved since I first came to Enniskillen, and I believe that there are still more helpful signs today. But that is the kind of society, with all its legacy of history, and its hurts and rights and wrongs as well as its kindnesses and considerations, into which Marie and all the others were born. Perhaps we were naïve, like so many others, in thinking that this legacy of misunderstanding would never touch us physically, and in such a shattering way as it has done. We thought it was enough to keep to the basic principles of trying to be good neighbours to all. But all those years I had a niggling fear that maybe I was in a minority of people who thought as I did. It was hard not to notice the strength of arguments on both sides, sometimes they were overpowering. I suppose, on reflection, I felt that Northern Ireland, despite our attempts at a peaceful existence on the surface, had deep underlying problems that would blow up some day, and blow up they did. In the end they led to a situation which blew a great, gaping hole right in the heart of our family.

CHAPTER TWO

Marie – the Formative Years

Marie Wilson was born at 3.25 p.m. in the Erne Hospital, Enniskillen on 29th April 1967. On that day I was not able to be with Joan, due to a meeting of the local Synod of the Methodist Church, but I was waiting anxiously for the call, which eventually came from my father, who had taken the message from the hospital. He was of the "Old School", and I remember his words, to this day. He said, "It's only a girl". I wasn't cross with him, but I was a little taken aback that anyone should still think that way. So that's how he broke the news to me – "It's only a girl". Some girl!

Marie was a good-natured baby, always smiling. The others gave her a lot of attention, and this helped her to develop quickly. Her mother, of course, knows all the little details about a baby and a young girl's life which most men either do not notice or cannot remember! So my recollections and memories of Marie are a joint effort between Joan and me. Joan and I had met some years previously at a local "soirée", or musical evening, in Enniskillen. I was attracted to Joan, whom I had never seen before. I asked someone, "Who's the lassie in the white dress?" They told me her name, and I made it my business to strike up an acquaintance. Eventually, the "lassie in the white dress" and I were married, and we made our first home in the tiny rooms over the shop in Enniskillen. We were young and happy, and well fit for the routine of nappies and broken sleep! By the time

Marie was born, we had moved from our home over the shop to our present house on the outskirts of Enniskillen, and Marie began life in a comfortable house surrounded by the love and warmth of a happy family.

Marie turned out to be a friendly soul. She loved people, and related well to everybody. I suppose that I spoiled her a bit, being the youngest, but Julie Anne and Peter were very good to her too. Peter was then eleven, and Julie Anne was seven. Both were thrilled with a new baby in the home. Peter remarked that he was glad there was a new baby girl, as she would be a good companion for Julie Anne! There is a temptation to remember only the good, and to make her out as very special. She was no saint, but just a lovely, high-spirited girl. She could be strong-willed, and a bit stubborn. Certainly she liked her own way. She would sometimes say to us, "I'm not going to be good just because you want me to be good". She would never put on a show, just for appearance's sake. She could not stand anything that was formal or strait-laced.

Marie was very musical, and this is largely due to the influence of her mother, who is a music teacher. She was very rhythmic, and could pick up tunes quickly. As early as the age of three she had her own small violin, and she would play "Twinkle, twinkle, little star". When she played, there was a twinkle in her eye too, because she knew that she was pleasing us. We all really enjoyed having Marie around, because in a way she was the "pet" of the house.

Joan recalls, "I made up my mind that I was going to 'enjoy' this baby, because with the first-born and the older children you are a bit anxious, and you sometimes feel that you are unable to cope. But by the time Marie came along, I had learned from the experiences with Peter and Julie Anne, and I was able to relax just that bit more. I remember vividly our pre-school walks every day, and Marie cycling or pushing a much-loved toy horse on wheels. She liked going up and down steps, and trying to open and to close doors. She also was quick to observe dogs and cats out for their morning stroll.

"We ended the walk by calling with Granny Wilson who was in failing health at this stage. She was always overjoyed to

see Marie, and she called her 'My little Ray of sunshine'.
I remember well the time Marie was sent to play school – but
she refused to stay! She protested that a boy had hit her in the
tummy, and since he did not know how to behave himself, she
demanded that a member of staff bring her home – which she
did. And she refused to go back!"

We thought that this might spell trouble for her at Primary
School, but when she went off to Enniskillen Model School in
September 1971 she settled well. Her brother Peter had spent
seven happy years at the school, and her mother had taught
there, in her first year after qualifying at Stranmillis Teacher
Training College.

Marie was fortunate to have a very experienced and excellent
infant teacher who was in her last year of teaching. We were so
delighted that Marie had this gifted lady during her first year
at Primary School. The seeds of language-training, a love of
reading, music and a wide range of interests were sown in
this classroom. Here she met Helen Glenn, who became one
of her closest friends. They were to go through many years of
school, holidays, and thrills and spills together, chuckling and
laughing as they went.

At home, Marie continued violin lessons with her mother,
but she did not take easily to the piano and always found it a
difficult instrument. She played in the Junior School Training
Orchestra, under the guidance of her mother, and she also took
part in an Orchestra Course at Benburb Priory. In her last year
at Enniskillen Model School she was involved in a memorable
production of "The Story of Stephen Foster". She sang, with the
chorus, such beautiful songs as "Jeanie with the Light Brown
Hair", and played in the school orchestra accompanying the
dancers.

As well as this musical background, Marie had taken part in
all school sports, and in the Girl Guides at Cathedral Hall. Her
experience at Primary School was fundamental. It had helped
her to qualify for Grammar School, to enjoy music and sport,
and to mix with other boys and girls. Although we were a bit
doubtful about her ability to pass the "Eleven-plus" exam, she
managed to get through. Perhaps she was borderline. I know

that her Headmaster had been a little apprehensive, but in the end it turned out all right. She liked going to the secondary school, Enniskillen Collegiate, which is situated just across the road from our home. She made her own distinctive contribution to the school, and became a Prefect, and eventually Deputy Head Girl.

At the Grammar School, her musical career developed further. During her first term the school produced "Fiddler On The Roof", and Marie played the part of the Fiddler. I well remember that we were in Cork during the weekend when she was given her Fiddler's costume. We phoned home to hear Marie crying and protesting about the "horrible costume" she was going to have to wear in the production. We managed to calm her and to convince her that if she wanted to act the part, this was the kind of costume which the Fiddler must wear. We heard no more complaints about the costume or the "silly hat"! Each night of the performance she climbed her ladder, sat up and played that haunting little tune which is so special in "Fiddler On The Roof". Little did we realize then how near our own story this theme would come, with its sense of sadness and loss. The whole show was a memorable performance.

School work, on the whole, was tolerated by Marie, who was not an academic. She enjoyed sport, but the school choir was most important to her. I remember how she helped to organize the choice of a new uniform for the choir. Again, there was frustration over this uniform. One day she came home from school, and threw down all the notes and patterns on the kitchen table shouting, "I've had enough! I cannot think what these girls want, they have changed their minds so often." Eventually they chose the choir uniform which is still a combination of green blouses and black skirts. Each time I watch it singing, I recall the headache and the heartache of a girl who loved singing in the school choir.

I daresay that this gave her a desire to sing in the choir at the Royal Victoria Hospital in Belfast. She was most enthusiastic about this, and it was a high point for her when we were able to watch the choir on local television. She sang her heart out.

She still kept up the violin. When she started Grammar

School she had reached Associated Board Grade Three, and she developed as far as Grade Eight, but, as always, the piano was a struggle. I think she enjoyed the violin because it enabled her to be part of a string quartet. When she went to the Royal Victoria Hospital, she became a member of the Studio Symphony Orchestra in Belfast, and we had the pleasure of going to the city to hear the orchestra play with the well-known Ulster musician Derek Bell, who has a classical background and who has also earned international fame as a member of the Irish music group "The Chieftains".

One of Marie's great school friends and the first violinist from the Erne Quartet, Lesley Coates, played with her that evening in the Ulster Hall when we listened to the Studio Symphony Orchestra. The girls really enjoyed making music together. Marie played in the Western Area Youth Orchestra, where she had the opportunity not only to share in music-making but also to meet with Protestants and Roman Catholics from over a wide area. And that also had an important bearing on her outlook and development.

At school Marie found languages quite difficult, but she loved her classes in Biology and Home Economics. We shall always remember the preparations for "O" and "A" Level practicals. The preparation of baskets, ingredients, recipes, flower arrangements, linens – everything had to be perfect! She brought her school training and her enthusiasm and her new recipes to our home kitchen. Mother's cooking was scrutinized and criticized. She insisted on serving the main course, and she pointed out forcefully that the plate had to look colourful. Oh, how the memories come flooding back.

She gave of her best to anything she joined. She had great inner depth, and even at Sunday School she used to ask the kind of questions which, the teacher said, hit him "right between the eyes"! I know that she was deeply affected by the television programme "Holocaust", which portrayed vividly the persecution of the Jews in Nazi Germany and in other parts of Europe, and this had a profound influence in her decision to become a Christian. She was a member of a local Youth Group which met on Sunday evenings, and where young people of all denominations met together to read the Bible, and to discuss the Christian faith.

In one sense she had always been a girl with Christian values. Many years earlier she had been very friendly with a local wholesale grocer, Richie Wilson, who, despite the surname, was not a relation. Richie was fond of children and he took Marie out with him in his van to do his Saturday rounds. This gave her a great insight into the life which revolved around little country shops. At this stage Marie was keen on playing that well-known children's game "I-Spy". In particular, she loved "spying" animals, and she was very fond of horses. During one Saturday morning she had "spied" about seven horses, but she wanted one more. She got down on her knees in the van and prayed that she would "spy" another horse. And sure enough, when Ritchie drove the van round the next corner, they both spotted a big, white horse. "What did I tell you," exclaimed Marie, "I knew that God would let me see another horse!" That's an example of a strong, child-like faith which Marie retained all her life.

However, I would not like anyone to think that she was a "holy holy" sort of a girl. For example, she was a great giggler, even to the extremes of being annoying. When she was in her teens we were on holiday in America, and we went to the local church. We listened intently to a lady soloist who began to "warble", and that was too much for Marie. She began to giggle, and you could see the very seat shaking with her laughter. It seemed as if everyone in this American church was turning round to watch this giggling in the Wilson pew!

She gave us lots of laughs, with her great, bubbly personality. What we miss most is her bursting in and saying "Mama" or "Dad", and opening her arms to enfold us. But my, she could be stubborn! Her mother used to get angry when she would not work at the piano. You could not drive her, and there was no way she would do something under pressure. She had to be led, and whatever she did, it had to be interesting for her. Many a time she and her mother fought over practising scales on the piano, and she would make a row and then stomp off to her bedroom. But if she did become involved in a row she would always come back again and say, "I'm sorry".

She was a good-natured girl, but she was easily bored. Our heads used to turn when she came bouncing through the door. "What have you planned for this evening?", she would ask. And then when we told her she might say, "Oh, I'm not doing that boring old thing!" So, in the end, we tended to let her get on with doing what she thought she wanted to do. She did everything with such eagerness. She used to become terribly bored with just chatting or merely going for a drive. She loved action.

As her father, I felt a special bond, again possibly because she was the youngest. It was the kind of relationship which you couldn't measure, and certainly she was not any closer to me than any other member of the family. I remember Marie, even as a toddler, meeting me in the hall of our house when I came in from work in the evening. She would say, "Hello Dad", and I would more often than not take her up in my arms. She was a good girl and lots of fun, with a great deal of love in her. The close affinity between us continued, right to the day she died. Every weekend when she was at home she would come into our bedroom and lie on the covers and chat to me about the events of the week. We were able to talk like that, on a similar wavelength, and, looking back, it was a most important part of our lives even though, perhaps like many another father and daughter, we did not think especially of it at the time. We got on well together, and that was more than enough.

She was sensitive, fun-loving, caring, full of humour, a girl with a big heart. We think her spirit is still around and it helps to keep us going. Joan and I can still see her at all ages and stages of her life, full of warmth and happiness. She did so much, she gave so much, and she still had so much to do and to give. And she packed such a lot into her twenty years, as if she was only meant to be with us for a short time. We all loved her, and she loved all of us.

CHAPTER THREE

The Gathering Storm

During the years when Marie was growing from a child into a young woman the situation in Northern Ireland became steadily worse. There was political deadlock, and constant bombings, shootings and killings, with all the human misery and suffering which they brought. Nearly every day there was a story in the newspapers and on radio and television about someone murdered or maimed, about families torn apart by violence, about fear and bitterness and reprisals. There was also a great deal of courage, and kindness and help for the victims of violence, but so often the bad news seemed to overshadow the good. Probably it was meaningless to those outside Northern Ireland, with its conflict rooted in centuries of misunderstanding, confrontation and division. Even in Northern Ireland it was difficult at times to understand what was going on, to comprehend the depth of the bitterness and to accept that the degree of savagery in our own corner could be as devastating as anything in any other part of the world. It just seemed to go on and on, despite the pleas for peace from successive church and community leaders. The security forces' spokesmen kept saying that their job was to "hold the ring" while the politicians tried to find a peaceful solution, but whether "the ring" was being held or not, the politicians seemed incapable of settling their differences and of laying a foundation for a peaceful, shared future. It would be a brave man who would try to work out the rights and wrongs of it all, or to say who or which side had a prerogative of truth or justification. But I always felt strongly that if we are going to find a peaceful solution in Northern Ireland we are going to have to live together and to learn to love one another, but all the while accepting our different traditions. I still believe we can learn to love, and play and talk as friends, and respect each other's beliefs, while agreeing to differ on certain basic points. So the choice was either to get up and go and leave the country, or try to live together as good neighbours. It seemed as if people of my generation had left a poor legacy for the younger folk, and that they were, and are, being left to pick up the pieces.

Our children were bound to have been affected by all of this, but in ways which were difficult to estimate. We helped to provide a secure, happy home, and they had a wide circle of friends including young people from both communities. But however hard you try as a parent it is impossible to protect your children from influences beyond your control and outside the immediate circle of home, family and friends.

Marie, like the others, was aware of the Northern Ireland troubles, from an early age. Probably her first direct experience was at the age of three during a Civil Rights march in Enniskillen. I remember it well, because it was on the day Granny Wilson died. There were a number of helicopters flying over and around Enniskillen. Marie asked, "Why are there so many helicopters?", and I'm not sure what answer we gave. There was so much happening that day, what with Granny's death and the general atmosphere of tension surrounding the Civil Rights march.

Marie's next experience of direct trouble was when she was about seven. A car bomb went off in High Street, Enniskillen, wrecking five or six shops and blowing out the windows in many of the others, including our own. I remember that everyone was very frightened. It was Marie's most direct experience of violence, and she could not understand why people should want to do such a thing. Eventually, however, she experienced the suffering of people in her own circle of friends and acquaintances. Richie Wilson, her friend in childhood who had taken her with him around the roads and lanes of Fermanagh in his grocery van, was killed in a car crash, and she was deeply upset. Later, the father of one of Julie Anne's close friends was murdered by terrorists. He, too, was a grocer but without any political background. He was a Sunday School teacher and much loved by all our family. Marie cried and cried. That family's anguish and grief was the most distressing we had ever seen, and it made a deep impression on all of us, including Marie.

In fact the trauma was so deep there was a niggling thought at the back of my mind. The future really looked bleak and I began to ask myself, "Maybe it's time to pull up the stumps and go?" This was something I had thought about, from time to time, and I'm sure that many other families did the same. So we began to talk about *where* we might go rather than *if* we might go. The natural place seemed to be Scotland, so I went over there on my own and talked to a few estate agents in a number of little towns here and there. I made it clear that I was thinking of setting up a business, and I found one place in a town called Cumnock, near Troon, that seemed a possibility. It was a busy mining town and seemed to promise a good future. The idea was to set up shop there, and bring over my own family. My son Peter, who by that stage was fully involved in our own shop in Enniskillen and was married with a young family, might come over as well, later on. The owner in Cumnock was keen to sell. I was impressed generally, and the figures seemed to add up.

On the way back home I drove from Belfast towards Fermanagh, and the nearer I got to Enniskillen the more I felt I was coming back among friends, to our family's roots, to the Golf Club, the Rotary Club, church and home, and all the familiar touchstones of life. And I realized that nowhere else in the world would match up to the setting of Enniskillen, with its lakes, its hillsides and its gorgeous scenery. So even before I turned my car into the driveway of my home I had come to realize that Scotland was not the place for us. We talked it over and as a family we decided to stay.

Of course we were still very much aware of the Troubles, and of the awful reality and legacy which they were creating, but life went on. And like many another family we believed that "It wouldn't happen to us". Yet all the time I felt that things were hardening, we were getting back to tribalism at its worst. And with this there was also a feeling of helplessness – what could

I do? And I was not the only one to think in this way. Like
so many other people we decided to let things ride, and in our
heart of hearts we hoped that the situation would improve, and
somehow it would all go away. There was another important
consideration – we had deep, deep roots in Fermanagh, we were
getting older, and only a terrific upheaval would have made us
pull up and go.

Somehow I don't recall having had any profound conversations on all these matters with the children, apart from the
question of maybe moving to Scotland. We felt that, despite the
Troubles, life was interesting and worthwhile, and things carried
on with their own momentum. Life was filled with so many
ordinary things: having people to supper, thinking about school,
business and church. Despite the Troubles, life was full, and in a
strange way it felt normal. Things were implied but never spelt
out. Like so many other Ulster folk we got on with living as best
we could, and despite the headlines about doom and gloom and
mayhem, life was for the most part surprisingly pleasant. This
is something which people outside Northern Ireland might not
understand, but if things had been as bad here as some people
think we might all have left long ago. But when things went
bad for an individual family, they were indescribably bad, as
we later found out.

Marie rarely talked directly about the Troubles, but like
the others, she could not avoid them. Early on she asked
me, "Daddy, what's wrong with Roman Catholics?" I replied,
"There's absolutely nothing wrong with Roman Catholics, why
on earth are you asking me that?" It was something which she
had picked up from outside. As she grew older Marie kept her
own counsel and she would never have come out with what
might be termed "hard-line" talk. We seldom talked religion
or politics, and if religion did come up it was usually in the
context of her church activities. The fact that we did not
discuss religion or politics in the Northern Ireland sense is
not an indication that we did not care. Of course we alluded
to it when certain incidents took place, but it was not a topic of
general conversation every day. Some people outside Northern
Ireland might find this hard to believe, but the Troubles are

not a question of Roman Catholics and Protestants shooting at each other from every street corner. The reality is much more complicated, and it is worth pointing out that the vast majority of Roman Catholics and Protestants are intent mainly on getting on with their lives and trying to live in peace. They are not continually at each other's throats, but on the contrary they face common problems of earning a living, raising their families and getting on with their neighbours.

Over the years Marie was aware that some people thought less well of Roman Catholics, but she never let anything like that interfere with her work or her life. She chose nursing partly because she got on well with people. One of Julie Anne's friends was training as a nurse at the Royal Victoria Hospital, Belfast and she listened to her telling about her experiences. One day I heard Julie Anne say to Marie, "Would you like to do nursing? You love people, would you consider it?" I cannot remember Marie's reply, but knowing the rapport between them her reply would have been something like "Mind your own business!" She was quite sure that she was not going to be a teacher, because she said that there were enough in the family already. For her Duke of Edinburgh Award she worked in a geriatrics ward at the local Erne Hospital. Here she had an experience of what one kind of nursing involved, because it was not easy to deal with geriatric patients. I felt that if she could stick at this kind of nursing she could do anything.

Marie talked to her careers teacher at school and discussed doing either business studies or nursing. She decided, however, to choose nursing and she prepared herself for an interview at the Royal Victoria Hospital. She was called in the month of February 1984, the weather was frosty, so she and her mother travelled to Belfast by bus. Her mother recalls two nurses on the bus that day, discussing in loud tones their hours "on" and "off" duty. Marie, apparently, was listening intently.

In Belfast they took a bus to the Hospital, along the Falls Road which had been at the centre of a great many disturbances. Marie's mother had remembered the Falls from her teacher-training days in the Fifties, but when she saw the same area some three decades later, her heart sank. Buildings looked

wrecked, paint had faded, and there were slogans on the walls
everywhere. They entered the Hospital and asked an ambulance
man the way to Bostock House, which is the nurses' home.
They followed his directions and joined the other apprehensive
parents and potential students. Her mother remembers looking
into a lecture hall and seeing a skeleton set up. Bells were ringing,
young student nurses were coming off duty and out of lectures.

Marie was clearly impressed by all of this, and she was
determined to do her training at the Royal. Nervously she hoped
that she would not make a mess of her interview. She didn't, and
a week later received a letter confirming that the Royal would
indeed accept her as a student nurse. Her dreams had come true.
She started training at the Royal in October 1985. She never
talked about specific patients, but we know that she made her
mark. When she died we received a letter from a priest, now
in England, whom she had nursed in the Royal. His letter was
one of the kindest we received. She was aware of the differing
backgrounds between Protestants and Roman Catholics, and
maybe that made her try all the harder as a nurse to be the
same to everyone. She often told us that she loved the "crack",
that is the repartee, with the Belfast men and women who have
their own quick, distinctive and sometimes devastating sense of
humour. She seemed to relate well with them.

I love the story which one of the lecturers told us in a letter
after her death. She hadn't mentioned the story to us. Apparently
she did a stint at psychiatric nursing. This lecturer was holding
a seminar with Marie's group and he was playing the part of a
man suffering from a severe depression. He painted a very sad
picture, with the implied question to the trainee nurses, "What
are you going to do for me?" He told us that Marie tried two
or three approaches to provide help but none seemed to work.
She appeared to have run out of ideas, and then she said almost
as a last resort to this "poor" man, "All I can offer you now is
my friendship". And, at that response, the lecturer told us he
had been very moved. That had never happened to him before.
Maybe that said something about Marie, and about the qualities
she brought to her work as a nurse.

Of course I was worried about her in Belfast. I said to her,

"Watch your step", and she replied, "Don't worry, Dad, I'll be all right." She was just like any other student nurse about the place, full of life but not looking for trouble. Sometimes, when we look back, it is hard to pick up the pieces or to understand how it all happened. There she was, working in one of the toughest areas of Belfast, and she was unscarred. Yet she comes home one weekend to Enniskillen and is killed by a bomb. It is hard to make any sense of it all.

If Marie had lived I don't know if she would have stayed in Northern Ireland. That was nothing to do with the Troubles, but rather the fact that she loved to get around. I was happy at the thought of her spreading her wings, seeing a bit of the world, discovering that there was more to life than the situation in Northern Ireland, and maybe in her own way spreading abroad some of the good news about her native Province.

A couple of months before she died, her mother and I spent a holiday in America. I am a keen golfer, though not necessarily a good golfer, and I met an American doctor with whom I shared a round. He is an extremely fine man, whose grandfather came from the area around Sligo. He had been a consultant gynaecologist who reckoned, at the last count, that he had delivered some twenty-seven thousand babies. We began talking about our families and I told him that Marie was a student nurse who, when she qualified, might be looking for a job. In fact not all of Marie's year found a job immediately at the Royal, so my consultant contact in the United States might have come in very useful. We kept in touch, and he offered to help as best he could. Sadly he saw later on television the news of the Enniskillen bomb, and he rang to try to comfort us. His words were extremely poignant, and I remember them clearly. He said, "I'll not be looking any more for a job for Marie".

That was after the horror of the bomb, but I look back on Marie during her last months, though we were not to know they were her last months, as a grown up, caring, responsible and respectable young woman who was happy in her work and in her play. In no way was she ground down or depressed by the Troubles. She had everything to live for, and she was the kind of daughter of which any parent would have been intensely proud. She was full of life, loyalty and love.

Her mother recalls two stories of Marie which paint her exactly as we remember her, showing both sides of her strong, outgoing character. "There was great excitement getting ready to go to St James's Palace to collect her Duke of Edinburgh Gold Badge. Marie wore a navy straight skirt, a navy and white check blouse, and a navy blue hat with a big leaf adorned with a little white rose. She had bought a new pair of navy blue high-heeled shoes to finish the outfit. Alas, before going for lunch, the heel of her right shoe cracked, and we were absolutely devastated. We thought that we had prepared for every eventuality, but now a broken shoe threatened to spoil the whole day. She tried to go to a shoemaker, but to no avail. Luckily the heel had not snapped off completely, and she was able to stand carefully in line during the presentation at St James's Palace, and reply politely and smile at the Duke of Edinburgh who presented her badge. Even then her sense of fun came out. There was an orchestra at the ceremony, and she gave me a sharp nudge as she said with a giggle, 'Mother, that orchestra is not playing in tune!' She enjoyed meeting the Duke of Edinburgh, but in no way would she have her picture taken afterwards. I suggested that it would be nice to have a formal picture taken but she put her foot down and said, 'No way, Mother, let's go back to the hotel'. And that was Marie. Once she had made up her mind there was no turning her. One of my great regrets to this day is not having a formal picture of Marie's Duke of Edinburgh Award. We do have a snapshot taken by a friend, but somehow it's not the same.

"That same evening in London she dashed off to see the musical 'Chess'. I paid through the nose for a ticket for her, but now I'm glad that I did. She came back so excited with a tee-shirt, a glossy brochure and a tape. It had been such a high day for her. Next morning she tore off to see the Trooping the Colour. She chatted to a London policeman, and she was overjoyed to see all the members of the Royal Family, including yet again the Duke of Edinburgh. She then suggested that we should have an open bus ride round London, which we did, and I was caught up in all her youthful excitement.

In the evening we went to see another popular musical 'Les Miserables', and we finished off the visit next morning with a service at Westminster Abbey. We listened to the organ and the marvellous choir, and we were wrapped up in the beauty of the music and the building. That evening we came back to Belfast. She went up to the Royal and I went on to Enniskillen. They had been one of the most beautiful and memorable few days of our lives."

"Not long afterwards we had another shared experience which I will never forget. It was the Autumn halfterm, and we decided to take a weekend break by the seaside. Marie was coming with me. We couldn't decide whether to go to Portstewart or Donegal, and eventually, we plumped for Donegal, partly because it was easier to reach from Enniskillen. It was perfect autumn weather: crisp, dry and sunny. We drove around the Fanad Peninsula which is one of the most scenic and beautiful places in the world. At lunch time we were hungry and searched around for somewhere to eat. We were delighted to find a little cafe, very clean and most inviting. The menu was good. Fishermen were chatting happily and partaking of the turkey and ham, and the fish of the day was on offer. The whole atmosphere of that little cafe delighted Marie. She sat at the window and enjoyed the beautiful scenery.

"Two lady golfers entered and one said to the other, 'Now, we must not order toasted sandwiches today. We have had them every day this week.' They perused the menu and seemed to look closely at each item on it. Finally they ordered toasted sandwiches, much to Marie's amusement!"

Marie was an adult woman now, no longer just a daughter to Joan but a close companion too, and Joan was looking forward to that deepening intimacy over the years which many mothers and daughters enjoy.

Joan was completely caught up in the matchless beauty of the sea, the mountains and the beaches, and gazed in wonder at its perfection. She was so moved at one particular scene of beauty that she spoke aloud to Marie the words of one of her favourite hymns by Isaac Watts:

I sing the almighty power of God
That made the mountains rise,
That spread the flowing seas abroad
And built the lofty skies . . . .

God's hand is my perpetual guard,
He guides me with his eye;
Why should I then forget the Lord,
Whose love is ever nigh?

Marie laughed and gently chided, "Trust you, Mother, to find exactly the right words for a time like this". They drove on, but as they travelled around Donegal, Joan was to tell me later, a great, secret loneliness came over her. She had a kind of premonition that this perfection would not last. She said nothing at the time, but as they drove back home to Enniskillen she was thinking that this was one of the great, priceless days to be treasured as long as she had breath in her body. Just over a week later, Marie was dead.

CHAPTER FOUR

Explosion

On the day that Marie died I had called her early in the morning to be on time for the Remembrance Day service at the Cenotaph in Enniskillen. I remember saying to her the night before, "I'll call you, and for goodness sake let's be away in time!" I like to keep a minute or two up my sleeve, because I'm a punctual kind of person and I hate to be late or to keep anyone waiting. Looking back on that day, I suppose you expect to remember every detail, but for some reason I find it difficult to recall breakfast, or getting out of the house. It was a cold, blustery sort of day and as we crossed the back yard my wife Joan called to Marie, "Have you an umbrella?" She replied, "Of course I have, don't fuss!" She waved goodbye and that was the last her mother saw of her until she lay dying in the Erne Hospital later that afternoon.

So Marie and I set off for the Cenotaph. I was glad to have her company because the others were doing other things. Joan is the organist at our local Methodist Church, Peter and his wife had their own family to look after, and Julie Anne was living on the other side of town. I was wearing my dark grey overcoat to keep out the wintry wind. I always called it my "funeral" coat because it was the kind of thing you wore to funerals around the country. There is something special about funerals in Ireland because a great many people attend to pay their last respects to the deceased and to his or her family. I believe that it's not quite the same in other places.

In Northern Ireland there is also a special atmosphere on

Remembrance Sunday. Many, many thousands of Ulstermen and women, and men and women from the Irish Republic, fought in both World Wars. Perhaps this is not always remembered in other parts of the British Isles. Nor is it always remembered in Northern Ireland that very many Roman Catholics from both parts of the island stood shoulder to shoulder with their Protestant colleagues to fight for freedom and, as they saw it, for a better world. The town of Enniskillen itself has a long and a proud tradition as the home of famous regiments like the Royal Inniskilling Dragoons and the Royal Inniskilling Fusiliers who won battle honours all over the world. On Remembrance Sunday we also think long of all those who have died in the Ulster Troubles during the past twenty years and more. I always make a point of going to the Cenotaph partly because of family – Joan's father lost a leg in the First World War – and also because I want to say at least once a year a personal thanks to my friends and others who went out to risk life and limb, some of whom never came back. I always think that there's a special poignancy about Remembrance Day in Northern Ireland because those who joined up did so voluntarily. They didn't have to, because conscription did not apply over here. Those kind of thoughts are always at the back of my mind on Remembrance Sunday, and they were also there in a kind of subconscious way as Marie and I made our way towards the Cenotaph.

We were approaching that area in good time and as we drove to a parking place past the War Memorial I distinctly remember saying to Marie, "That Cenotaph looks very exposed, I sure hope the security forces made a good check last night." Perhaps in my mind's eye I was thinking of the bands coming up to the Cenotaph, of the noise, the marchers, the colours. But at that moment the whole place looked bleak, and maybe because of the contrast to what we expected in a few minutes' time with the bands and the marchers coming along, it looked particularly vulnerable.

Whatever I said to Marie, I remember that she didn't reply at that point. We parked in the nearest car park and made our way back up the direction we had driven, towards the War Memorial. By that time some more people had gathered.

We made for the spot where I always stood, beside the old community building. It was the kind of structure which provided shelter from the rain and the prevailing winds. I suppose we were about thirty-five to forty feet away from the Cenotaph itself, so we were able to get a good view of everything. As we walked to that spot I was behind Marie and I recall saying to myself, "That lassie is strong and well-built." She was good at skiing, and tennis and badminton. She liked sport and she loved physical exercise.

By that stage she had been away at the Royal Victoria Hospital for two years, and it crossed my mind that not many people would immediately recognize her, apart from knowing that she was "Gordon Wilson's daughter". I spoke to ten or twelve people I knew and bade them "Good Morning!" When we eventually arrived at the place where I usually stood, I said to Marie, "Can you see all right?" She steadied her gaze, looked at the scene in anticipation of the parade making its way to the Cenotaph, and said, "Yes, this is fine." From the moment she spoke, it was only about fifteen seconds until the bomb went off.

The "Bang" was the first thing I heard. The thought went through my head, "My God, that's a bomb going off", but this was a sharper sound, not all that loud, but sharp and sharp enough to tell me that the bomb was not at the far end of town but near enough to be very close. I don't know how anybody else was responding at that moment, but I turned as I stood and I managed to look over my right shoulder. Marie was on my right. I must have realized that the bomb had gone off behind me, and I remember seeing the wall beginning to crack up. This all happened in a split second but it seemed at the time as if everything was happening in slow motion, like a television replay.

Then, it seemed to me I was pushed but not "shot" forward, and I seemed to come down on my face. This must have been happening very fast, but at the time it didn't seem at all like that. It was like being pushed down on my face in slow motion, it was extraordinary really. Certainly it was all happening, or seemed to be happening, slowly enough to give me time to think yet again, "My God we're in a bomb blast . . . . but it can't be, not here, not at the Cenotaph on Remembrance Sunday!"

At this point there was no sensation of noise that I can remember. There was no screaming, no shouting, but a kind of limitless, eerie silence. Having realized that the wall behind me was falling, I said to myself, "One big slab from that wall on the top of you boy, and that'll be the end, that'll be it, it'll be goodbye!" But when the wall had finally finished collapsing, there was only the sound of the gravel stones trickling down after it. And my mind flashed through the message to my spreadeagled body, "The big one didn't get you after all!"

By that stage I was flat on my face, and I must have been pushed on my mouth and nose, because my glasses had come off. I realized that we were buried beneath several feet of rubble, but there was a chink of light coming through and I could sense the rain water on the stones. I thought that my glasses had been lost. Normally I can see very little without them, but in the middle of all that I was able to see sufficiently well to spot the glasses and somehow to put them back on again, with one hand. It seemed like a miracle at the time.

With my glasses I could also see some blood trickling down a stone and I knew then that I was cut. I had been taking an anti-coagulant drug and I was afraid that my blood would start to flow freely. As it happened, it was only a graze, and later the wound required only three or four stitches.

All the time I was lying there trying to find my glasses and put them on, still lying down on my mouth and nose, the noise level was increasing. Just after the blast there had been a sinister hush, a terrible quietness. And then the noise came, roaring and resounding and penetrating the several feet of rubble above us. There was shouting and moaning, and screaming, and yells of agony, until it all built up into a terrifying crescendo. At that stage a small voice inside me said, "I'm not too bad", and if that sounds like self-interest, it was also pure, basic human instinct, and a deep sense of thankfulness to be alive, even in a fix like that.

Yet, equally quickly, the still, small voice began to niggle away at me, "What about Marie, where is she, is she hurt? Let me get to her!" The explosion had thrown me forward, and my right arm was trapped. It later transpired that my shoulder had been dislocated, and therefore I had very little room for movement or manoeuvre. At that point I realized that it was not possible to get out, certainly not without help from outside. But all through the screaming and shouting there was the urgent question in my mind, "Where's Marie, is she hurt, is she trapped, is she alive?"

Then, almost by magic, I found my hand being squeezed beneath that pile of rubble, and I knew it was Marie. She gripped my right hand and asked, "Is that you, Dad?" I could hardly believe that she was here, after all, lying beside me in the rubble. But the noise outside, up there if you like, was increasing, and with all the screaming and the din and noise, we had to shout louder and louder to make ourselves understood to each other. So we yelled, as best we could, amid the partial darkness, and the noise.

I shouted, "How are you, Marie?" She replied, "I'm fine." My heart skipped a beat, with relief. But then, suddenly and terribly, she screamed. I knew that there must be something awfully wrong for her to scream like that. Again I asked her, "Are you all right?" And again came the reply, "Yes". But there seemed to be a bit of hesitation in that "Yes". A little later she shouted to me, "Dad, let's get out of here." I replied, as best I could, "Marie, there's no getting out at the minute. We are trapped beneath all this rubble, but not to worry, they'll soon find us. There's a lot of people around, and they're certain to be digging down to us already. We've got enough air, there's a bit of light, and with God's help, we'll survive."

But then she screamed again. It was her second scream. I became desperately concerned about Marie's condition. I could not, and I still cannot, understand how she could keep reassuring me that she was fine and yet, in between these messages of reassurance, she was screaming. Whether they were screams of pain or of terror I'll never know. I didn't know how badly she'd been hurt, but she was a very sensible girl of twenty, she had been trained as a nurse, she would have known how to cope. She must have known she was hurt, and badly hurt. And I know now that she had been losing a great deal of blood by that stage.

It must have been four or five times I shouted to Marie, "Are you all right?" But then, suddenly, her voice changed, she sounded different. She held my hand tightly, and gripped me as hard as she could. She said, "Daddy, I love you very much". Those were her exact words to me, and those were the last words I ever heard her say.

After that her hand slipped away, and we lost touch. By that stage the others had reached me, and they began hauling me out of the rubble. It had been hell in there, but the even worse hell of facing the aftermath was only beginning.

CHAPTER FIVE

Aftermath

When they came to dig me out of the rubble I knew that I must have been in a state of shock or that maybe I had fainted, because after Marie's last words to me there was a period of about ten minutes which I could not, and still cannot, account for. I must have lost consciousness but I was not aware of doing so, or of regaining my senses. The rescuers began by trying to haul me off my face in the rubble but I had to say to them, "Wait, boys, my arm is caught". Another voice repeated hurriedly what I had said and warned the others, "Careful, his arm's trapped! He seems to be in pain." So they worked with me more gently, which was quite something considering the pressure those poor fellows were under, and they slowly and carefully got me to my feet. I said, "I feel all right, boys", but none of them would have known me because I was covered all over and grey with dust. I said, "Don't worry about me, but for God's sake try to get my daughter in there, she's under the rubble. She was lying beside me." I then realized that I was able to move my limbs, and two of the rescuers helped me towards the little parapet at the Cenotaph where I sat down while they set off to try to find Marie.

At that point I saw a man walk towards me and I recognized him as a member of the Ballyreagh Silver Band which had been scheduled to play at the Cenotaph. Once the explosion took place everyone piled in to try to help. There were soldiers, policemen, bandsmen, civilians and anyone and everyone who could lend a hand. However the bandsman did not recognize me, though I knew him partly because as outfitters we had supplied the uniforms and partly because Joan's father had been a member. I was dazed, and those details seemed important at the time. There was someone I felt that I knew and to whom I could relate. Then I saw another man, a friend called Ronnie Kemp, who was the Principal of a local Primary School. I thought, "Here comes a friend I can lean on", but he walked right past without recognizing me. On reflection I'm not surprised he did not recognize that dusty and dishevelled figure at the base of the War Memorial, but at the time I couldn't work out why Ronnie had not stopped by my side. Later I was told, of course, he hadn't recognized me and that he was rushing to give help at another part of the bomb site.

All the while, I was wondering, "What has happened to Marie?" I could see nothing but people running about amid the shouts and the screams, and I gradually realized that I must be in some state of shock. Again and again I thought about Marie, and I reasoned to myself, "Surely if she's no worse than I am she would be out of the rubble by now, but where on earth is she?"

Then some more rescuers came to my help, and I told them about the severe pain in my shoulder, so someone got me a wheelchair, and took me in a police car to the Casualty Department of the Erne Hospital. The doctors would not give me a painkilling injection until they had set my arm, so I was in considerable discomfort. The scene in the hospital was chaotic. There were the dead and the dying, and the injured, and relatives coming in tearfully, and dozens of people rushing about. Staff who were off duty and had heard either the explosion itself or the news about it, were coming in voluntarily to help, and setting up emergency procedures and generally getting involved. There was not much time for anyone to think. Somebody wheeled me into a side room and told me to wait. Then I noticed a man with a clipboard and pen and I recognized him as Norman Hilliard, a senior hospital official. He was working his way towards us. People were either standing or lying, or sitting. There was a bit of moaning and crying, and all of us were more or less dazed. Norman Hilliard seemed to be counting heads and making a list of the injured, so when he got to me I asked, "Any word of Marie,

Norman?" He said, "I don't know, Gordon, she's not on the list, but we'll let you know."

The next person I saw was the Roman Catholic clergyman Monsignor Sean Cahill. He must have driven straight to the Hospital. We were on first-name terms, and his visit, for me, was most comforting. He asked, "How are you Gordon?", and I replied, "I need all the help I can get". We both held hands, and I think we cried, and he said a short prayer. I asked him to look out for Marie, and he promised he would. He was glad to see me because I was the first injured person he knew, and I was very glad to see him. He helped me and I like to think that maybe I helped him too.

Then I recognized the Church of Ireland Rector Dean John McCarthy, together with Dr Robin Eames, the Archbishop of Armagh. I remembered that the Archbishop had been due to preach at the Remembrance Day Service at the local Cathedral. I did not know Dr Eames personally, but I tried to make a little light of the situation. Dean McCarthy said, "Archbishop, he's not one of 'ours'. Mr Wilson is a Methodist!" But I replied to Dr Eames, "I might not be one of 'yours' now, but you were once one of 'ours'!" I was referring to the fact that Dr Eames' father was a Methodist, like me. The Archbishop seemed to appreciate the attempt at humour. He smiled, and we chatted and shared a prayer. I found it very comforting, and helpful too. After he left I said to myself, "A sound man is Robin Eames". He, too, promised to look for Marie.

All the while I kept thinking of Marie and I asked everyone I could to try to trace her. Then our own minister, the Reverend Tom Magowan, arrived. We talked and prayed together, and he set off to try to find Marie, as well. By this time I had been sent to an area for minor injuries. That is not to say they were trivial as such, but compared with some of the others they were comparatively minor. The doctors diagnosed my dislocated shoulder, put my arm back in, and gave me a pain-killing injection. Then I was taken to the physiotherapy room, which was a kind of clearing station, and soon afterwards my family began to arrive, and Julie Anne was the first. She said, "Thank God you're all right, Daddy." I asked her, "Where's Marie?", but she did not know. The fact that no one came back to tell me of Marie's whereabouts, despite all my questions, made me begin to fear the worst.

Meanwhile, news of the deaths and terrible injuries began to filter in. Somebody said, "Poor Johnny Megaw's dead", and the enormity of the tragedy began to hit us. His death was the first which was mentioned to me. The carnage and sense of despair at that time is hard to describe, but I cannot praise highly enough the staff at every level. They had enormous problems dealing with the whole situation, and they coped extremely well. There was a great sense of teamwork between those on normal duty and those who came in to help. Everyone did his or her bit. At that stage I was still dazed, and it is hard to remember clearly the detailed sequence of events. But my wife, Joan, has total recall of all that happened from her perspective, from the time that Marie and I left the house. And while I was lying injured in the hospital and unaware of the greater drama of Marie's last moments in another part of the building, Joan saw it all, and she has an agonizing story to tell in her own words.

*

I waved goodbye to Gordon and Marie as they drove away from home to the Cenotaph. I turned back into the kitchen and thought "I shall see them after church." We were looking forward to having lunch with Peter and his wife, Ingrid at their home. The front door bell rang, and Peter came in with our granddaughter Judith, (who was two years old). I was and am always overjoyed to have a visit from my two granddaughters. The elder girl, Eloise, was in Sunday School with her mother, Ingrid, who was teaching a class in the Methodist Church. Peter, who is Secretary of the Sunday School, had a quick cup of coffee with me and left to go down to the church. Judith remained with me, and I was to bring her down to church at 10.45 a.m. to join her mother, father and sister. When Peter left the house I heard a thud and I said to myself, "What was that? Was it Peter closing the car door very loudly or was it a bomb?" In a few minutes Peter returned and told me that a bomb had gone off at the Cenotaph. We were both frightened, as we knew Dad and Marie had gone there. I phoned Julie Anne and told her the news, and she set off for town from her home on the outskirts of Enniskillen. I gathered Judith into my arms, placed her in the back of Peter's car and we set off on our first search.

I tried not to transmit my dread and fear to little Judith, but her face told us she knew that things were not normal. We drove quickly to another war memorial at the bottom of the town but we were not allowed by the security forces to go up towards the main Cenotaph, which was blocked off. Peter parked the car, and said he would go and glean some information, if possible. He begged me to sit in the car with Judith and try not to panic. We sat there until he returned ten minutes later, but he had little news. He had seen and talked to various people but they knew nothing of Gordon or Marie. As I looked toward the Cenotaph it looked as if a building had disappeared, and the statue of the soldier on top of the war memorial was now etched against the skyline. That was a different landscape entirely. Something seemed to be very wrong.

I tried to figure out where Gordon and Marie might be. Perhaps they had not reached the Cenotaph, I thought. Perhaps they had gone home. If people were injured, Marie would be sure to help; I hoped she would remember her First Aid and do it correctly. At that point I never dreamt that she or Gordon would be caught up in the bomb. Peter and I decided to go home and see if Gordon and Marie had returned there, or, we hoped, they might ring from somewhere down town. When we arrived home there was no one around, nor did the phone ring. What could we do next? We thought they might have gone on to church, so to the church we drove. There was no sign of them. I went into the church hall to tell my daughter-in-law the news. She had not heard the explosion. Julie Anne now joined us, and she and Peter decided to go to the hospital. Our minister, the Reverend Tom Magowan, arrived at the church and I told him Marie and Gordon were at the Cenotaph. Several Girls' Brigade members were now arriving from the Cenotaph, where they had been waiting for the parade. They were crying, shaking and distressed and I was very frightened when I saw them. I said to one of the little girls I knew, "How bad are things down there?" She said, "Mrs Wilson, it is dreadful". She cried and cried and I asked, "Did you by any chance see Marie and her dad?" She just shook her head and said, "I saw them taking up their position to watch the parade".

I was really very frightened now. Mr Magowan asked me if I wanted to sit quietly in church until I heard some news. I preferred to play the organ as I wanted to occupy myself rather than sitting thinking and fearing the worst. Mr Magowan conducted the service. Twenty minutes after it started, I realized I would have to go out and leave the organ as I was becoming overwhelmed by anxiety. I could neither listen nor concentrate. Then a member of the Ulster Defence Regiment appeared. He was one of our own members whom I knew very well. He beckoned to me and I went over to him. He whispered to me to come along with him because he had received a message that Gordon was in the Erne Hospital with a broken arm. One of the nurses from the church choir followed me, and accompanied me to the church door. Peter was waiting in his car and brought us to the hospital. He knew Dad had a broken arm, but still knew nothing of Marie.

At this stage I was crying out for Marie and fearing for her safety. We entered the hospital at midday. I shall never forget the scene. I had never seen anything like it before, and I hope I never shall again. Most people were quiet and shocked; some were crying bitterly, some quietly, others were comforting people. I was brought to Gordon. He was sitting in a wheelchair, with his shoulder dislocated and with a cut on his forehead. Julie Anne was standing giving him all the support and comfort she could. Someone put a cup of tea into my hand. Gordon's first words to me were, "Any news of Marie?" Then he burst out crying. "The pet told me she loved me." I was slowly trying to piece the story so far, but I did not understand what he had said. At this stage I realized that a wall had fallen on them. I learned they had been under rubble, and I was absolutely horrified. I also learned there were many people missing, including Nessie and Billy Mullan, whom I knew and loved. Johnny Megaw was dead. I could not believe what I was hearing.

Gordon was brought for X-ray and then taken away to have his shoulder put in place. When he returned, I sat by his bed. At 2.30 p.m. Peter and Julie Anne came to us to say that Marie was in theatre. That was the first real news we had of her. A policeman, whom they knew, had brought her bracelet, ring and necklace to them to identify. I'm not sure where he found them. When we heard this news we held our breath, and we hardly dared to speak. An anaesthetist, a specialist from the Erne Hospital, came to Gordon's bedside and asked to speak to us. The curtains were drawn round the bed, and we heard the first news that Marie had very severe injuries. She had had a cardiac arrest when she was brought to the hospital. Her pelvis was broken and she had internal injuries and profuse bleeding. They had given her twenty-four pints of blood. As I listened, I felt my legs growing weaker and weaker, and all hope draining from me. We knew now that Marie was very, very ill. Gordon said to the specialist, in his own direct way, "Sir, I think you are telling us there is no hope for Marie?" The specialist replied, "We are fighting for her life, and we are still hoping". We thanked him. He left telling us that they would keep us informed.

Some time passed. Another doctor and nursing officer, whom I knew very well, asked Peter, Julie Anne and me to come to a little office. This doctor again warned us that Marie was gravely ill. He mentioned the injuries and internal bleeding. He warned us that she would never walk again and that she would have brain damage. At this stage, I prayed out loud saying, "Oh Lord, Thy will be done". We returned to Gordon's bedside, and gave him the latest report. We were all beginning to prepare for the worst. Our next call was from a nursing officer to say that Marie was out of theatre and in Intensive Care. We were on the ground floor with Gordon. He was still in bed and in agony. Peter, Julie Anne and I set off to Intensive Care upstairs. I walked, and begged God to give me strength to cope. I met a lady doctor whom I knew. She had lost her twenty-seven-year old daughter during the year, through cancer. She took me in her arms and whispered, "Please God, you won't lose your dear daughter too!" I thought of the great sorrow she had gone through and how brave she had been.

When we got out of the lift, Sister met us and told us that Marie's heart was still beating, but it might stop any minute. We turned into the room. The specialist who had been one of the many who fought for her life in theatre was standing beside Marie's bed. He looked at us sadly, and shook his head. I could not believe that the girl who left our home at 10.20 a.m. so full of life and vitality was lying there with her life ebbing away. "Why? How? Was I having a dream?", I asked myself. Sadly, the answer was "No". My darling Marie was dying. I kissed her and I shall always see her eyelids flickering, to my dying day. Sister whispered very gently, "Mrs Wilson, Marie's heart has stopped beating". Julie Anne took my hand and said, "Mum, it is better this way". I could only utter, "The Lord gave, the Lord has taken away. Blessed be the name of the Lord." I knew I had to lean hard on the Lord now; He was my only strength. I had to go down and tell Gordon that his darling daughter was dead. I kept going back to look at Marie. I am sure I walked in and out of that little room six times or more, until Sister gently and very lovingly reminded me I had a duty to go downstairs, to tell Gordon.

I understood, but I cannot remember making my way downstairs. I do recall Gordon saying to me, "How is Marie?" I had to put my arms around him gently and say, "Our child is dead". He cried out, "Oh my God, is Marie dead?" Our minister the Reverend Tom Magowan was right by the bedside. He prayed and supported us. He cried. He was in such a state; we could not believe what had happened on this Remembrance Day. I remember seeing my poppy lying on the floor under Gordon's bed. Our next-door neighbours had kept vigil all afternoon. Sadly and silently they received the news but they could not believe Marie Wilson was gone. They loved her and she them. They had watched her grow up. It was all so awful.

Eventually Gordon was allowed to go home. Our minister wheeled him to Peter's car. I did not want to go home because I was sick at heart with the thoughts of home without Marie. It was just too much to bear. In the car we didn't say much. There wasn't much to say, but Gordon in his own way said all that had to be said, "It's going to be different, from now on, for all of us. The next two or three days will be very difficult, but let us try with God's help to muster as much dignity and strength as we can." With that Peter drove us out of the car park, and we all went home. All of us, except Marie.

CHAPTER SIX

Shock Waves

When we arrived home, the house was in darkness. It seemed very quiet. Within minutes the phone and the doorbell were ringing. Friends who lived away from Enniskillen and who had heard about the bomb on the radio and television, were enquiring about our safety, while at the same time neighbours were arriving to express their sympathy and to offer their help. The news of Marie's death had spread quickly. In the next few hours we were shocked and shattered to learn that ten others had lost their lives and that many had been injured, some very seriously. The enormity of the disaster was beginning to dawn upon us, as we realized that other homes and families were facing the same plight as we were.

More and more people came to our house and the downstairs rooms were soon crowded. We quickly reached a stage where visitors were standing in the hall or sitting on the stairs. Neighbours and friends took control of our kitchen and made sure that everyone who called was given tea and something to eat. Many had brought cakes and sandwiches, knowing they would be needed. This is not to suggest that anybody was hungry, but the very act of serving or drinking tea or coffee helped to ease the tension and to break the ice on what might otherwise have become very awkward conversations.

So on the early evening of Marie's death our home was crowded and everything was being taken care of in a respectful, quiet and yet a purposeful way. There were mounds of sandwiches, cakes, everything you could imagine. This was very important, for it gave Joan and me an opportunity to go around and say a few words of thanks to people and to share our grief with those close to us. There were very few tears, because there was no time for crying. It was a question of putting your best foot forward. There were so many people who called and paid their respects, and on some occasions there was a queue right out to the gate of the house. All of this was very demanding in terms of nervous energy, and we were only human. Sometimes when there was a breather, someone would bring us to meet another caller and I would feel, God forgive me, "But not again". Yet it all helped us greatly. It was not only tough for us but it was also tough for those who had come to see us. There's not a great deal to be said in a situation like that.

It all added up to a "buzz" about the house, but that was good for us. It meant that we hadn't time to think, or to dwell on things too deeply at that point. Even though we knew in our head, so to speak, that Marie had "died", it really hadn't sunk in. Our hearts went out to the other families of the dead and injured. I said to Joan, "We must go and visit these people and share their grief", but in fact we didn't get around to doing so because there was so much else happening all around us. They were the same, because everyone had his or her own grief to bear and to share, and so many things to sort out. However, all the families met each other within the next couple of days.

Sometime during that evening I decided to take a little break and to go outside for a breath of fresh air. Two young men came up to me, and one of them I recognized as Charlie Warmington, a Producer in the BBC. Though based in Belfast he was an Enniskillen man, and his mother lives just half-a-mile from us. Charlie introduced his companion, who was another BBC journalist, Mike Gaston. They asked if I would like to give my version of events for BBC Radio, and I said that I would.

By the middle of that afternoon there had been public messages of condolence from Buckingham Palace and 10 Downing Street. In a statement the Queen had said, "I was deeply shocked to hear of the atrocity which took place in Enniskillen today and of the innocent victims who were sharing in the nation's remembrance. My heartfelt sympathy goes to the bereaved and the injured in their distress."

Mrs Thatcher told reporters outside 10 Downing Street that the explosion had been a "blot on mankind". She said, "Every civilized nation honours and respects its dead. To take advantage of the people assembled in that way was really a desecration. It was so cruel, so callous, that the people who did it can have no human thoughtfulness or kindness or sensitivity at all. It was utterly barbaric." The Irish Prime Minister, Mr Charles Haughey, spoke of his deep horror at the bombing. He said, "I know that I speak for every decent Irish man and Irish woman in expressing the anger and revulsion we feel towards those who planned and executed this criminal act of carnage against the innocent people gathered to commemorate their dead."

The condemnation was widespread. The United States President, Ronald Reagan, expressed the "revulsion" of the American people and wrote, in a letter of condolence to Mrs Thatcher, "It is a very cruel irony that such a deed should be done on a day of remembrance". Pope John Paul II expressed "profound shock". The Enniskillen bombing was becoming a big international story; it was one of those horrific events which stops the civilized world in its tracks. However, when the BBC reporter Mike Gaston asked me to say a few words that night, I was unaware of the extent of the shock waves that were going out from Enniskillen. He was very courteous, and after one or two "warming up" remarks, I answered his request, "Tell me what happened this morning". As best I could I described the events at the Cenotaph, and I talked about lying under the rubble with Marie, and her squeezing my hand, and of her last words to me, "Daddy, I love you very much". Then I went on to say, "The hospital was magnificent, truly impressive, and our friends have been great, but I have lost my daughter, and we shall miss her. But I bear no ill will, I bear no grudge. Dirty sort of talk is not going to bring her back to life. She was a great wee lassie. She loved her profession. She was a pet. She's dead. She's in Heaven, and we'll meet again. Don't ask me, please, for a purpose. I don't have a purpose. I don't have an answer. But

I know there has to be a plan. If I didn't think that, I would commit suicide. It's part of a greater plan, and God is good. And we shall meet again."

That was all I said. Mike Gaston had asked me a question, and I had given him a straight answer. That night the interview was broadcast, and the next morning as well. Personally I had no inkling whatever of the effect it would have. Much later, after all our visitors had gone, I finally got to bed, but I could not sleep. Nor could anyone else. It was the longest night of our lives. We tried to talk, but we had few words to offer each other. We walked about the house, upstairs and downstairs. We held hands and bodies, as we sobbed and cried. We grieved in our loss with long periods of uncontrollable agony. We thought the dawn would never come. We prayed again and again for others and for ourselves, that God would give us the strength and the Grace to meet the days ahead.

We met the new day early and were determined to try to face up to whatever it might bring. I went to the hospital for a physical check-up and then to the Health Clinic nearby to seek advice from my doctor. I could not make up my mind whether or not to look at Marie's mortal remains in the mortuary. I had not seen her since just before the bomb. Should my last memory of her be as I saw her then – full of life and vitality, or as she now was, in her coffin? My doctor strongly advised the latter and I am glad now that I heeded his wise words. I had feared that my final memory might be one of Marie's remains and that this would dominate all my other memories of our happy days together. Mercifully, this did not happen. My memories of Marie are predominantly of the good times, and my last sight of her was no more or less than saying goodbye to her mortal remains. The Marie I had known and loved was no longer there.

When I came back to the house around 10.00 a.m. there was a camera crew at the front door, and another one in a car, parked nearby. There was no way I could not talk, having given the initial broadcast, and I had no thoughts to the contrary. The fact of suffering was there for all to see. Some people had reacted to my radio broadcast and had said, "He's in a state of shock, he can't mean what he says!" Even though I was indeed shocked, and although my voice had broken with emotion once or twice during the broadcast, I knew exactly what I was saying. And I would like to think that if the same thing happened again, I would have the grace to use the same words.

On the day before the funeral I gave interviews from just after 10.00 a.m. until late in the afternoon. There were reporters, cameramen and sound recordists from all over the place. They were from Belfast and from Dublin, and there were several from London. There were also reporters from international news organizations. Those which did not send reporters took the "clips" from other broadcasting stations, by arrangement. The pressure was so great that by 4.00 p.m. Julie Anne put her head round the door of our livingroom and said, "For God"s sake, Daddy, tell them to go. Surely you've had enough."

Some people have since asked me, "How did you endure such pressure? Where did you find the energy to keep on talking? Did you feel any kind of purpose in talking to so many media people, or were you rather dazed by it all and carried along on their tide of questions?" The answer is simple. I gave the first couple of interviews because I was trying to be courteous and I did not want to turn people away. I lacked experience with the media and I thought that each interview would be the last. But when you have talked to one or two reporters you cannot in all fairness refuse the others. Of course I was tired, and throughout that day one part of me was saying, "This is all going too far." But another part of me was thinking that the bombing was so horrible that people should be told about it, at first hand. Perhaps subconsciously I was also saying that if sufficient people were shocked by what happened in Enniskillen this might help to make them say "Enough is enough", and to begin to bring this country to its senses. While at no time, then or since, did I regard myself as a "spokesman" for Enniskillen I moved from being merely courteous to realizing that this story had to be told. Even though friends and family were advising me to ease off, I felt that my interviews were achieving an important purpose and perhaps ultimately for good. At no point was I "dazed" or "carried along" on the tide of questions. At all times I was in total control and I felt that the story should be told as simply and as lucidly as possible. Some of the media portrayed me as "The Voice of Enniskillen" but that was not of my doing. I saw myself as *a* voice but not *the* voice of Enniskillen.

All the while I was conscious that many friends and acquaintances had come a long distance to see us and that I was not giving them all the time which maybe they deserved. But I also thought that it was important to facilitate the news reporters and their colleagues.

As I was doing those broadcasts I was becoming more aware of the extent of the suffering. There were other families who had lost relatives, and who were facing their own grief and trying to come to terms with what had happened to their loved ones. There was Willie and Nessie Mullan, Edward Armstrong, Jessie Johnston and her husband Kit, Johnny Megaw, Samuel Gault, and Mrs Georgina Quinton. Young Julian Armstrong, who had been standing near the Cenotaph at the time of the explosion, lost both his parents, Wesley and Bertha, who had been beside him. Six of the dead were members of Enniskillen Presbyterian Church, and that was an awful tragedy for that one congregation which, in the words of its minister the Reverend David Cupples, was totally "stunned and shocked". According to the papers there had been sixty-three injured altogether, and about twenty had remained in hospital. One of the most heart-rending stories of all was that of a local headmaster, Ronnie Hill, who was badly injured and who has lain in a coma for years. There are many "voices of Enniskillen", and each with its own story to tell. It just so happened that my voice was carried by the media in a way which personalized the grief which we all felt.

On that Monday morning, Charlie Warmington of the BBC rang me from Belfast. He asked if I had any idea of the "buzz" which had been created. Apparently hardened reporters were in tears or near to tears when they heard the broadcast. Charlie warned me that there would be many more requests for an interview, and how right he was! The story simply would not go away. I'm no fool and I knew that if, for example, ITN were sending a crew all the way to Enniskillen they would almost certainly want an interview, and at least use a part of it. But I truly thought that this would be just another interview of a relative who had lost a loved one in the Ulster Troubles. There had been many before me.

Looking back at it clinically, it must have been what they call "good television" and radio, but the impact was totally beyond my control. The story was being transmitted around the world and I could do nothing about it. The whole thing began to frighten the pants off me. There were all sorts of implications and I knew that very quickly I could be out of my depth. But the one thing that really sustained me was the enormous comfort that Marie's last words had been words of love, and throughout all that time and through all the interviews I was given the grace to stay on that plane of thought.

Eventually, on the day before the funeral, the media packed up their microphones and cameras and left us. I then had to turn to meet hundreds of people who had called with us. The family were glad to see the media leave, if only for the simple reason that it left available another room for visitors! People were not only crowded on stairs, they were outside the front door and even pressing against the hedges because of the lack of space inside. The time came, however, when we had to leave the crowds and go to the mortuary to bring Marie's remains to the church, where there was a short service with scripture lessons and prayers. As I was leaving the church the Reverend Tom Magowan, our Minister, told me that the media had asked if they could set up their cameras and lights in the church to cover the funeral the next day. I said, "This will be a Thanksgiving Service in God's house and I do not want it to become a media circus." I am glad to say that the media kindly took the point.

On the night before the funeral we got a little sleep, but we were tense and anxious about the next day. We had to face the ordeal of burying our daughter. Surprisingly I still had not realized the extent of the media interest, and as we walked from the house there was another camera crew recording every step. The service was held in the Methodist Church in Darling Street, and it was packed. There were television cameras and bright lights in the vestibule but not in the church itself. It was a matter of taking one step at a time, and of getting on with the service. It was not easy for any of us. There was a great deal of emotion and an overwhelming sense of Marie's presence, among her friends. There were public figures, doctors and nurses from the Royal, some of her old school chums, friends of Joan and mine, and many people from Enniskillen and from further afield who had come to pay their last respects. The Reverend Tom Magowan gave the address and Marie's uncle the Reverend Dr Henry Plunkett, as one of the officiating clergy, read a portion of Scripture. Mr Magowan had a very difficult task to say the right thing on behalf of everybody, and he did it very well. We deliberately chose to make it a service of thanksgiving for Marie's life, rather than a service of mourning for her death, and Mr Magowan reflected that sentiment in his address.

*

"My first words must be addressed today to Gordon, Joan, Peter, Julie-Anne and the family circle. You have been much in our prayers and thoughts since the outrage at the War Memorial at Belmore Street in this town. This has stunned and shocked our whole community. The repercussions of which has sent shock waves across the world and brought the world's press and media to our doorsteps. But the repercussion I am addressing now is the one which has shattered your family circle, and Marie, your treasure, dear and precious, has gone from us to be with the Lord.

"On behalf of the congregation of this church and circuit that cradled her in its bosom and nurtured her in her faith in Jesus Christ as her Saviour and Lord, I extend our deepest heartfelt sympathy. The presence of so many here today from every part of the community, across the religious divide, is a testimony to the great wave of love, compassion and caring that is surrounding you as a family at this time, and indeed all the families who have suffered loss and injury.

"Marie Wilson was born on 29th April 1967, at the Erne Hospital, Enniskillen, and baptized by the Rev. Alan Hanna, who is sharing in this service today, a former Superintendent

Minister of the Enniskillen Circuit. She comes from a family with a distinguished record of service in the Methodist Church, and attended Sunday School and worshipped here in this church . . . Marie was an enthusiast, and anything she took up she pursued with vigour. She glowed with life, and had a real caring personality, and brought sparkle into all our lives. She had a real caring concern for people.

"Marie loved her family. It was a wonderful day for her when she was bridesmaid at her brother Peter's marriage to Ingrid. She later made great friends with her two young nieces, Eloise and Judith. But her caring reached beyond her family circle. It was her caring, her willingness to take time and show love that led her towards nursing as her vocation. In this she was encouraged by the Careers Teacher, Miss Kate Doherty. She entered training at the Royal Victoria Hospital, Belfast, and had just started into her third year of training to be a Registered General Nurse. Being of such a radiant, lively personality she had immediate rapport with all the patients who came under her care. Her friendliness, sense of humour, and sincerity won for her many friends among staff and students. When she came home from the R.V.H. on days off she went through the place like a whirlwind, so full of life and vitality, packing every moment with activity. There was cheeriness and real genuine concern for not only her family, but also her many friends in Enniskillen and beyond.

"I received her into full membership of the church, and Marie epitomized for me the Scripture verse that says, 'Be ye doers of the word and not hearers only'. It was a blessing to know and to be a minister of Marie Wilson.

"This family has received so much in the brief twenty years of God's love through her caring, loving personality, that Gordon and Joan, Peter and Julie Anne can say, 'the Lord gave and the Lord has taken away, blessed be the name of the Lord'.

"You tell me Marie Wilson is dead, and presently we will lay to rest her mortal remains with much love.

"I saw the spirit of Marie in the Casualty Department of the Erne Hospital.

"I saw the spirit of Marie Wilson in the wave of compassion and practical caring that crossed over the religious divide as a shattered community came close together in love and succour for the bereaved and injured. Though we sorrow today, we do not sorrow as people without hope. The secret of the radiant, vital life of Marie came from her personal faith in Jesus Christ as her Saviour and Lord.

"On behalf of the family I wish to express thanks to the staff of the Erne Hospital – Mr A. McKibbin, Consultant Surgeon, Dr W. Holmes, Consultant Anaesthetist, and the team of doctors and nurses who fought for her life in theatre.

"Mrs M. Egan, Director of Nursing Services, and all her nursing staff who rose so magnificently to the crisis, and all those who came in to offer their skills to the injured at the scene of the outrage, and at the hospital.

"And at this service, Mr David Asater, Head of the Instrumental Department, Western Youth Orchestra, who is our organist, the string quartet, and trumpeter Stephen Magee.

"Our service today is a Service of Thanksgiving for the life of Marie Wilson.

"Shining through this service is the note of triumphant faith and victory over all that would seek to separate us from the love of God in Christ Jesus our Lord.

"No, friends – neither life nor death, nor principalities, nor powers,

    nor famine or nakedness
    peril or sword,
    nor height or depth,
    and, may I add, nor bomb outrage, nothing shall separate us from the love of God in Christ Jesus our Lord.

"This is the victory even our faith . . . and that is why I will go on loving, go on caring, go on preaching, and ministering, and go on in hope, for our hope is in Christ who loved us and gave Himself for us.

"Will you go on caring, loving, hoping, as Marie did?

"We commend the family to the love and comfort of our Father God, and all the families in this town who mourn and have suffered loss and injury at this time.

"The Lord gave – and the Lord has taken away.

"Blessed be the name of the Lord."

On the way out, as Joan and I held hands walking down the aisle behind Marie's coffin, I spotted in the congregation the local Bishop of Clogher, the Very Reverend Brian Hannon. As we walked past he reached out, held my arm, and whispered, "Well done!" That was a very supportive thing to do, and it came just at the right time. The funeral was not as difficult overall as we feared it might be. We did not make fools of ourselves, and the whole family coped. As we made our way to the cemetery we passed the Presbyterian Church where they were holding the funeral service for Edward Armstrong. It was a forceful reminder that we were not the only ones suffering that day.

We laid Marie to rest in the Enniskillen graveyard. The final prayers were said and then the Blessing, and we left Marie's mortal remains in that freshly-filled grave. It was just over two days since she had stood by my side, young and lovely and alive. And now she was gone. We went back home to try to face whatever the future would hold for all of us.

CHAPTER SEVEN

Gestures of Love

It dawned slowly, and painfully, that Marie had gone. There was no blinding flash or a point in time when the truth sank in. It was like someone slowly lowering a blind inch by inch, rather than shutting the light out suddenly to enclose the darkness. Even today there is still a kind of darkness. It comes in patches. Some days are better than others, but then there are times when it is totally bleak, and we feel as if we are back to square one. Sometimes it's "one step forward and two or three backwards", but we persevere.

It is hard to remember what we did on the day after Marie was buried. There were so many apparently ordinary things to be done, clearing up details of the previous three days, seeing people, and generally trying to keep our heads above water. It had been a very, very difficult time, and both Joan and I were shattered, as were other members of the family. It was hard to sleep. The doctor prescribed sleeping tablets for me and there was the pain from my injuries, as well as the deep emotional and psychological scars, which were still raw.

Because of the injuries, I found it difficult to cope with some of the simplest things, and Joan had even to wash my hair. Every time she did this, she realized yet again the extent of the bruises, the discoloration, and the fact that she had to wash away a great deal of the dust and dirt from the bomb which had matted my hair. "My poor dear", she cried, "look what they have done to you." She said that she couldn't understand how one human being could hurt another like that. Yet there was nothing for us, but to go on. We had to look outward.

Someone told me that there would be a memorial service for the bomb victims, in the local Roman Catholic church of St Michael, on the Thursday night. I felt that I should go, to show personal solidarity with and compassion for all those who had lost loved ones, from whatever background they were.

On the day of the memorial Mass I contacted some of my Methodist friends and talked it over. I said that I would be happy to go on my own because Joan was caught up with people visiting our house and could not get away. People still came to see us, morning, noon and night. A local Methodist minister, the Reverend Derrick Haskins, said, "I'll go with you Gordon", but I said to him, "Derrick, do you realize that if you go to a Roman Catholic service you might run up against some opposition down here in Fermanagh? You might have to pick up a few pieces and take some 'stick' as well." He made the distinction between going as an official representative of the Methodist Church and as one of the men who had ministered to me. He agreed to come, and I knew that I would feel at ease in his company. I was not in great shape physically, with my arm bound up, but I rang the Parish Priest and asked him if there would be any objection to our going and he said, "Certainly not". I asked him to keep us a couple of seats near the back, because I did not want to walk up the aisle in the condition I was in. There was no way that I could stand or go an hour earlier to get a seat.

The arrangement was made and Derrick and I went along to the chapel. When we arrived the church was packed, and television cameras seemed to be everywhere. We were met by church officials in the vestibule and we were shown to the seats which had been kept for us near the front, and not at the back of the church as I had expected. As we walked up the aisle I was amazed that people were clapping, and everyone got to his or her feet. I knew that Cardinal Thomas O'Fiaich, who has since died, and the local Bishop were to be at the service, and I assumed that the applause was for them. I looked up to the front to watch for their arrival, but they were not yet there. Suddenly the penny dropped that they were applauding Derrick and me! I was totally flabbergasted. I couldn't believe my eyes or ears.

Soon afterwards, the Cardinal and the Bishop arrived, and the Mass began. As the service progressed I had a feeling that I had never experienced in quite the same way before, nor have I since. The service was solemn, yet comforting and deeply moving, with everyone being totally sympathetic. I felt that I was in the very presence of God. At the end of the service it seemed that everyone came to shake my hand. As much as I appreciated this, I was dazed by it and afterwards in my home, as I watched it on the television news, I could still barely take in what had happened to me. The phone rang and I was told that the Cardinal was in the Parochial House, and I was asked if I would like to meet him. There was no doubt in my mind that I would. It wasn't every day that an ordinary man, and a Methodist to boot, had the opportunity to speak to a Cardinal. Shortly afterwards, a car pulled up outside our house and I was taken to the Parochial House. We talked for about fifteen minutes, and I felt more at ease in the Cardinal's company that I had expected. We both made a conscious effort, or perhaps an unconscious resolution, not to become involved in the "political bit", or "Protestant-Catholic" attitudes. He did not speak on behalf of the Catholic Church, nor did I speak on behalf of Protestants. It was an informal, friendly conversation and we talked "man to man". The Cardinal offered his sympathy to me and my family, and we also talked about the losses of the other families as well.

Later that week, some people asked why I had gone to the Catholic service. There had not been much time to think about motives or reasons for going, but something inside told me that the Catholic people of Enniskillen were making an important gesture to all the families of the eleven who had died. They were saying in effect, "We are terribly sorry for your trouble". They were willing to pray for us, and to extend the hands of friendship and love. They were not merely saying, "We are sorry for your trouble", they were saying in an even deeper sense, "we are truly *sorry*". I think that the Cardinal himself said something like that publicly, during the same week. I felt very deeply that this warmth of response from my Catholic neighbours was important and that I had to share it with them. It was not a profound gesture on my part, and as far as I am concerned, I would do it all over again.

It is important to make the point, however, that the Reverend Derrick Haskins and I were not the only Protestants in the church that night. Afterwards other people told me that they had never seen so many Protestants in the local Roman Catholic church. They were moved to go, and they went. The Catholics were offering friendship, and that was most important. The eleven who had died were all Protestant, and I felt that the Protestant people in Enniskillen were willing to receive any gesture of friendship, little or large, that was offered.

Afterwards I took a bit of "stick" for going. A minority of people felt that I had sold out my "Protestant heritage" by going into a Roman Catholic church at all. Maybe that's a reflection on the sort of hardening there is in Northern Ireland, or at least hardening among some people in Northern Ireland. I took the criticism and I survived. The attitude of hostility from a minority of Protestants made me very sad. I felt that I was right to go, and I still do. It was a natural response, a very human gesture seeking solace and healing.

There were other very important church services around that time. The Enniskillen bombing had a profound impact in the Irish Republic. The Irish Premier, Mr Charles Haughey, had spoken of the "anger and revulsion" of every "decent Irish man and woman" in expressing their feelings towards those who had "planned and executed this criminal act of carnage against the innocent people gathered to commemorate their dead". This sense of shock and solidarity was symbolized by a one-minute silence throughout Ireland on the Sunday after the bombing. On the same day, Mrs Carmencita Hederman, the then Lord Mayor of Dublin, came with the signatures of scores of thousands of ordinary Irish men and women and children in a Book of Condolences which she presented to Enniskillen. She tried to make a speech which she had carefully prepared, but she broke down, and that very act of breaking down told us more of her heartfelt sympathy and solidarity, and that of the many people she represented, than a thousand well-turned phrases.

One of the most moving services of all was held in St Patrick's Anglican Cathedral in Dublin a week after the bomb. Public and community leaders from all over Ireland had gathered to pay their respects to the Enniskillen dead and the injured, and to their families. The preacher was the Right Reverend Brian Hannon, the Anglican Bishop of Clogher, whose diocese includes Enniskillen. He had been on the scene quickly on the day of the bombing, and it was he who had given me a steadying hand, which I so much appreciated, as I walked down the aisle behind Marie's coffin. During the Dublin service, which was televised nationwide, Bishop Hannon preached on a text from Ephesians, "Christ is our peace", and his words have that stirring ring of truth which must never be forgotten. He spoke these words:

Thank you for being here this afternoon. Thank you for the wave of prayer and compassion that has surrounded those injured and bereaved in last Sunday's tragic atrocity in Enniskillen, and for the new determination by so many to say to all our fellow countrymen – No more of this. From whatever source it comes, and in whatever cause, aggressive or retaliatory, such bestiality is a blasphemous rejection of the God who loves us, and in whose image we are made. Rather than protecting or achieving any human right, it is an abdication of our right to be called human. Nothing in Ireland north or south can justify such actions. Nothing can absolve us individually or corporately from the responsibility to see that it cannot and will not continue. And may God forgive us all individually and as communities for any action or attitude of ours that has contributed either to the violence or to the bitterness and anger that leads to it. The world has grown weary of our so-called "insoluble" problems; of our bombings and our shootings; of our dropping concrete blocks on peoples' legs in punishment, or hacking off their fingers in captivity; of our robberies, our protection rackets, our hostages, our burnings or our intimidation; and of course of our astonishing capacity for talking to everyone around the world except each other. But somehow Remembrance Sunday 1987 in Enniskillen has added not only a new dimension of horror, but also a new dimension of hope.

There must be few people in these islands and far beyond who are unaware of how it happened. People gathering in the vicinity of the Cenotaph to remember lives sacrificed in two World Wars and throughout our troubled years. The bomb behind a wall. The explosion with all its horrific consequences. Bystanders blasted against the railings trapped under feet of falling masonry. Ten dead in a matter of moments. Pensioners and parents killed, side by side with teenagers miraculously left alive. A young nurse holding her father's hand, with final words of love for him as she lost consciousness. The five-hour battle for her life conceded later at the Erne Hospital.

Because the Presbyterian Church is just around the corner from the Cenotaph, it's easy for worshippers to attend the wreathlaying and then come back to church; but not that day. Six of that small congregation were dead and others injured. In the cathedral half a mile away the explosion had been heard. News of what had happened began to filter through to us. No Remembrance Day parade would come; just the four British Legion standardbearers and the bugler, shaken but stalwart. Many of the congregation were already gathered. The Primate was to preach. But as the grim details reached us, he and the Rector went straight to the hospital, while I led a short service to pray for all caught up in the tragedy and to ask for God's help and guidance for all who would minister to them.

At the hospital staff at every level and from every background appeared in strength. Their caring ministry was total; saving life, easing pain, helping fellow human beings. Clergy and church-workers of every denomination were comforting and praying with patients and relatives. Some casualties were hard to recognize, and some were in no condition to speak. Helicopters began to ferry patients needing specialist treatment to Altagelvin or to the Belfast hospitals. I had met one man in the street, who was looking for his mother. She'd been a hospital sister in Enniskillen some years back, and had been decorated for nursing service in the last war. That morning that Donegal woman had been in a proud fuss about which side to wear her medals on. Later her handbag was brought to the hospital. Derek recognized it. And then we went to identify her body lying side by side with the others under clean white sheets in the make-shift mortuary. There was no shouting, no hysterics, just a bewildered acceptance that this was life and this was death in our province.

Later that afternoon I returned to the Cenotaph. Most of the rubble had been cleared. The emptiness was of the soul as well as of the street. Just a cluster of newsmen, microphones and cameras. Their presence at times was oppressive, but some have become good friends, and without them the world would not know what personal faith can bear, and what community support has begun to achieve. Can anyone forget Gordon Wilson's description of his daughter Marie's last moments of conscious life? Can anyone doubt the forgiving spirit, or the determined confidence that God's purpose of new life personally and for the community could be found in and through this crucifixion? Gordon spoke for many in Enniskillen, and the world has listened. Some of the most hardened wept with us, and hearts began to soften. Marie's service of thanksgiving in Darling Street Methodist Church set the tone of the week. The sparkle, vitality and caring of the young nurse shone through. The compassion of the congregation, both Protestant and Catholic, and the confident Christian hope expressed gave us heart.

We've moved from Church to Church, paying our last respects to committed Christian church men and women, praying for the bereaved, supportive of those still critically ill in hospitals. At Sister Quinton's funeral I found myself singing, "Praise, my soul, the King of heaven", and meaning it. Among the bereaved and injured I have met so little bitterness; just a deep sadness, complemented by an amazing Christian maturity and grace. The reaction from far and wide has been staggering. Local too. No one will forget the standing ovation given by the immense congregation in Enniskillen's Roman Catholic Church at their commemorative service, when Gordon Wilson came in to kneel in prayer. I believe that that ovation was of sympathy and appreciation for all those who have suffered in this crime against humanity, and who have demonstrated dignity, restraint, an astonishing Christian spirit, and a concern for the community and for the future of our land.

But is this any different from any of our other ghastly nine day wonders? I believe it is. After twenty-four hours I said publicly that this could be the catalyst, the cross-roads, the turning point in the history of our troubles. Another word for a turning point is conversion, and conversion describes a change of direction in a person's life involving mind, heart and will. If it is a religious conversion it involves a decision to let God's way take over from mine, in fact to let God be God. There are signs of such change. The change of mind can be seen most obviously in a growing belief that violence leads only to pain, chaos, division and despair. The change of heart is experienced in growing revulsion at the inhuman and deepening obscenities of violence, realizing that we are being dragged into a quicksand of amoral depravity. And the change of will is being felt in the growing determination of individuals, churches and of our states that violence must not be allowed to win. Mind, heart and will; all the ingredients of conversion, of a turning-point and a change in direction.

That change of direction in our province must also be seen in moves to create a new future together rather than let anyone divide and destroy us; it cannot be achieved of course without genuine acceptance of one another as fellow human beings, fellow citizens and fellow Christians. In the broader context do you believe that no matter what their political aspirations or ambitions, all others in this land are also human beings created in the image of God? Do you believe that the others who live in this island, no matter what their origin, have a right to stay here and to share responsibility for the state in which they live? Do you believe that members of other Christian denominations can be just as genuine and true followers of Jesus Christ as you are? In other words, since I am a member of "The Church of Ireland", should I assume that we are the Church of Ireland, and it is simply a pity that everyone else doesn't know any better? Or if you are a Roman Catholic, do you assume that you are the Catholic Church and that therefore everyone else is obviously non-catholic? Or if you simply say, "Ah, but I'm a Christian", do you assume that everyone else who hasn't qualified your way is not?

And when it comes to identity – what are the tests for being acceptably Irish? How many generations back should we go? Maybe we believe in Hitler's doctrines about purity of race, or a South African system of green, orange and coloured? Now, our family, although Northerners, feel truly Irish – their four grandparents go back (1) to the Norman invasion with Strongbow, (2) to gravestones dating back to the 1600s in Co. Kildare, (3) to the Moriartys of Dingle Peninsula, and (4) to the Scots-Irish of County Antrim. And yet we all travel perfectly happily on British passports, and have no identity crisis. Could it be that there are many kinds of Irish (north and south), that we can actually benefit by one another's existence, that we can enjoy the rich variety of culture, that we will gain much if we have the courage to become truly pluralist societies, and that the political questions of sovereignty will only be solved when we have accepted each other and each other's right to exist? The really difficult border problem in this island is not the three-hundred mile invisible line across the land, but the much more divisive border in the hearts and minds of people. We need each other in the North. North and South, we need each other's mutual support rather than pressure. But in any agreement made for joint action, we need consultation with and the co-operation of all the parties involved.

So how can our Enniskillen experience help us to move forward? Well it could be the week to which historians look back and say, That was the week when Ireland, North and South, made the conscious decision to reject utterly the bomb and the bullet as a solution to any of our problems; the week when our two states made the conscious decision to create united, inclusive and pluralist communities within our respective boundaries, so that mutual respect and trust might grow between us.

It will of course remain only wishful thinking unless we grasp the opportunities that have opened to us this week, creating trust and building bridges in the community at every level. Every citizen must know he has a responsible stake in the state of which he is part, but also that he will be held accountable for that trust. Policing and security must be accepted as a joint responsibility for all sections of the community committed to democracy, which means of course that both sections of the community must actively take on and identify with that responsibility, and in protecting people either in Northern Ireland or in the Republic, it is quite obvious that this can only be achieved by mutual support on both sides of the border.

As I said earlier, the future for either part of this island depends on united communities, co-operation and trust. Enniskillen has opened doors in that direction. St Paul tells us in his letter to the Ephesians that Christ is our peace, that he has broken down the barriers; that he can reconcile us both to God in one body through the cross, thereby bringing the hostility to an end. Let's take him at his word, because we have seen proof in Enniskillen that good is stronger than evil, and we thank God for what he is doing in and through his people in every church. Thank God for those who have given their lives in innocence and in service to the whole community. By our attitudes and actions let's see to it that their sacrifice is not in vain. "In all these things we are more than conquerors through him who loved us."

It was a very powerful address and the questions Bishop Hannon posed still hang in the air. There were many tears shed in the Cathedral that day, and, quite incredibly, the audience broke out in spontaneous applause at the end of the Bishop's address. He was very moved himself by the whole atmosphere, and later confessed that he had walked back from the pulpit in tears. It was as if the whole land was mourning with the families of the dead and with the injured and their families, and at the same time mourning for all the terrible atrocities and tragedies, for all the hurts and heartaches, and the misunderstandings and divisions among all the peoples of this island, North and South. It was truly a nationwide day of mourning, and it was a most moving and memorable experience, which those of us who lived through it will never forget.

There was another service which had a special poignancy for Joan and me. Within days of the news of Marie's death reaching the Royal Victoria Hospital, there was a suggestion to hold a memorial service. It was decided to hold a joint act of worship, and this was extremely important to us, in that Marie would have approved, as we did, of an act of worship which brought together people of different backgrounds and persuasions. The service became "An Act of Thanksgiving for the life of Nurse Marie Wilson and of reflective memory for those who also died in Enniskillen on Sunday 8th November 1987". It was conducted by the hospital's Chaplaincy team, including both Roman Catholics and Protestants, on Sunday 22nd November. We could not be present, because we were physically and mentally exhausted, but we were with them in spirit. The theme of the "Act of Thanksgiving" was partly "the building of bridges of understanding and the breaking down of barriers and mistrust which are the most effective memorials to those who have died".

The address was given by the Methodist chaplain, the Reverend Sydney Callaghan, and he spoke eloquently and movingly. Towards the end he said, "In paying tribute to Gordon Wilson, let us not be insensitive to the burden that the mother-heart bore too, in that Joan Wilson shared those closing hours with Marie. And we must not overlook that agony and anguish that any mother will understand in a way that no father can fully comprehend. But in talking to Gordon about this service he expressed his gratitude for it though they cannot be present with us and he said, 'will you please remember all the people'."

I was glad that Sydney mentioned Joan because she had been so much in the background. It so happened that I had been propelled forward to face the media, but I was always conscious of and dependent on the support of Joan. There have been and are days when she is my only support around the house, and anything she has had to tackle she has done far better than I could. Her grief is just as deep as mine. We both share it, and also suffer separately, and she would be the first to admit that she did not have to face the extra burden of my personal injuries or having to face the media. The whole thing has brought us even closer. Throughout all the tragedy we have stood together, and that has been one of the things that has helped us both to pull through. The church services, and the Act of Thanksgiving at the Royal Victoria Hospital were moving, important and memorable, and necessary as a means of sharing together and of allowing people communally to share their grief. But it is in the home, and now the often empty home, that we need the strongest faith and the greatest sharing of all.

CHAPTER EIGHT

Friends, Family and Neighbours

Early on we learned what it was to have good friends and neighbours. The poet John Donne wrote, "No man is an island sufficient unto himself", and we found how true that was. In Ireland there is already a well-established tradition of friendship and neighbourliness, which might not be a feature of life in other places. This neighbourly concern in Ulster is not intrusive, but more an awareness in general of what is going on next door without being nosey. This is often evident in sickness or incapacity when special help is offered and accepted, or even in simple things like somebody saying, "I hope that we did not disturb you by banging the garage door late last night!"

We have been fortunate to enjoy the friendship of neighbours who know when to offer help, and when to leave us to ourselves. So when an enormous trauma like Marie's death overwhelmed us, our friends and neighbours were truly wonderful. After the explosion the news travelled quickly, both by word of mouth around Enniskillen and also through the news flashes on the media. Within a short time it was headline news throughout the British Isles and all around the world. One of the most admirable reactions came from my sister, Joan Plunkett, who heard the news in her home at Lisburn, and immediately set off in her car for Enniskillen, which was a two-hour drive away. She had an idea that we were involved, and she came down as quickly as she could to offer her help. Our next door neighbours, George and Edna Young, went to the Erne Hospital immediately. They heard the news and they stayed at the hospital throughout the afternoon. They were a great comfort to Joan, Peter and Julie Anne, though I did not see them myself. The Youngs had lived beside us for several years, and their daughter Helen and Marie had been good friends. Helen took it very badly when Marie died, and she still does not find it easy when she comes home from university in Edinburgh. George Young is the Principal of Marie's school, just across the road, and he knew her well. He wrote a beautiful tribute for the Enniskillen Collegiate School Magazine, which was published a few months after the explosion;

> The death of Marie Wilson in the bomb explosion on Remembrance Sunday brought a deep sadness to all of us in school who knew her. The response of her family, characterized by their decision that the service on the day of her funeral should be one of thanksgiving for her life rather than one of mourning for her death, is a fitting lead for us all in this school community, in our reaction.
>
> While she was here with us, Marie was the embodiment of integrity, goodwill, enthusiasm, a warm regard for everyone and a brisk no-nonsense cheerfulness. Self-pity played no part in her make up, and her example ensured that those around her did not succumb to it either.
>
> Whatever she did – and she was willing to tackle everything – was always given her total and best efforts and, like Oliver Goldsmith, she touched nothing she did not adorn.
>
> We are all the poorer for her passing, but we are grateful for what she gave us and for the memories she left behind.

Our other close neighbours, across the road, were Derek and Molly Hart, and they were the kind of people who would water your flowers when you were away on holiday. Derek was the man to consult if you had a leaky pipe, or anything practical that needed fixing or doing. It was Derek, for example, who drove Joan and Julie Anne back to our house on the day of the funeral, while the men went on to the graveside for the final committal service. With neighbours like the Youngs and the Harts you could not go far wrong, whatever your need.

On the night of Marie's death they were in our kitchen helping to keep things running smoothly and to make sure that all our visitors had a cup of tea or coffee and something to eat. They saw to it that we did not run out of the essentials, and that meant a lot to us, especially later on when we realized how much they had been doing. At the time we were so busy meeting people that we had no time to think about the little things like hospitality which, if they are not properly organized, can become no longer "little things" at all. The contribution of our neighbours, in this and so many other ways, made all the difference.

Our daughter-in-law Ingrid, Peter's wife, was also a tower of strength. She virtually lived in our house during the week of the funeral, and the fact that she was able to do so was due in no small part to her mother "Nanna Wood", who looked after our grandchildren Eloise and Judith, who at that time were little more than toddlers. Throughout that whole period Ingrid and Peter and Julie Anne were marvellous. They did all the right things and they did them well. It cannot have been easy for any of them. Peter and Julie Anne, as Marie's brother and sister, felt the tremendous pain of her loss. Ingrid not only liked Marie as a sister-in-law, but she loved her as well, and she felt the pain of loss equally. The strength of a united family is an enormous comfort on such an occasion, and we appreciated ours very much.

We also appreciated the presence of those who had made an effort to be with us, even though they would not have been expected to have done so. For example, a farmer and his wife from Enniskillen came to see us, partly because she was a nurse in the Erne Hospital and she shared the bond of nursing with Marie. She felt moved to come and see us, with her husband, and we felt the better for her visit. There were others, like the ladies who knew Joan from her work as a music teacher travelling around local schools, and who came to see us all the way from Omagh and Londonderry. The depth and range of goodwill was unbelievable.

On the Sunday morning after the funeral we went to our local Methodist Church. It was not an easy occasion because the last time we were there, it was for Marie's funeral service. To my surprise, and dismay, I noticed that a television cameraman had set up a camera near my seat in the church. I asked him politely to move it, and he kindly did so. It was bad enough having to take my seat in the church again and to try to pick up some semblance of privacy and normality, without having to face a television camera as well. However, my enduring memory of that service was the presence of a man and his wife and family who had travelled from Dublin to share with us. They belonged to a Dublin prayer group, and they felt inspired to come North and to convey the sympathies of the group to us and to all the other victims of the explosion. It was a lovely thing to do.

One of the most unforgettable visits was that of Mrs Norman Ross, whose son Stephen had been injured in the blast. She was quick to come round to see us, even though her son was being taken to Altnagelvin Hospital in Londonderry with severe facial injuries. People can be totally selfless at times of great grief, and I am sure that the families of the other victims could tell much the same story as ours. It was impossible on the night of the explosion to meet the other families, but we tried to go to as many funerals as we could. Even today it is hard to paint a vivid enough picture of Enniskillen during that dreadful time. On one day alone there were three different funerals taking place in different churches at roughly the same time, with all the attendant cameras and reporters and mourners. On the day after Marie was buried we went to the funerals of Billy and Nessie Mullan, and the next day those of Bertha and Wesley Armstrong. So, taking into account the service on the Thursday evening in the Roman Catholic chapel, I was able to share in a broad spectrum of the local acts and services of remembrance.

In a way it was like being part of the grief of one large family, because we knew so many of the victims and their relatives. Wee Johnny Megaw was a man who spent every Sunday afternoon visiting the sick in hospital, and he was well known and appreciated for this. Nessie Mullan used to work in our shop. She was a fine woman, and a first-class employee. Her husband, Billy, was a quiet, soft-spoken man who was an Elder in the Presbyterian Church. He was, as we say in Northern Ireland, "one of the best". I knew Mrs Georgina Quinton as a customer, and there was something about her, and the way she spoke, that would have made you realize she was a nurse. She had an air of caring, which came across to other people. Bertha and Wesley Armstrong were members of our own church. Wesley sang in the choir, and when Joan, my wife, held a choir-practice, Wesley used to lead them in prayer. Bertha was very much the wife and mother and was a centre of strength in the family. I felt particularly sad for their son Julian, who lost both his parents in the explosion.

We had great support from the local clergy, who themselves went through a most difficult time, and yet found the grace and the strength to reach out to others. The welfare authorities were also most supportive, and I was especially grateful to Cruse, the Belfast-based branch of an organization which helps people to deal with bereavement. All of these people and organizations gave the relatives as much help as possible, right from the start. After the explosion some of the welfare people were up at the hospital, trying to be of assistance with bewildered, distraught and in some cases screaming relatives. Within the next few weeks we were all brought together for collective meetings where we were able to share and to get to know one another better. They were sad occasions, not surprisingly, and it was not easy for any of us.

It was the people with whom I had shared the ordinary things of life, such as our regular morning cups of coffee, who gave great practical help in the most important of ways. About a week after the funeral one of my "coffee mates" phoned me up and said that I had better come and join them, for there was no point in me brooding on my own. At that point I could not even drive, so he ferried me regularly to the coffee shop and back. My lunch friends, a different group, rallied around as well. We talked about the most mundane things – about who had the best golf scores the previous Saturday, or who in the local district was ill, or the cost of living. These apparently mundane subjects were a wonderful therapy because they pointed the way back to a sort of normality that had been shattered by the bomb and its aftermath.

It was the same with my Rotary Club friends, and also with my golfing companions. I'm not a very good golfer, but I'm terribly keen, and that makes up for a lot! My local club is at Murvagh in Co. Donegal, just across the border from Fermanagh. That is the one place in the last few years where I really had the feeling of being away from it all. My weekly game of golf, with a regular partner, has been a great solace. There's something wonderful about walking over God's green grass amid marvellous scenery, and being away from people and able to switch off. Golf, of course, has its own challenges and frustrations, and there was a time in my life when I took my golf, and myself, too seriously! It has taken maybe twenty years for the penny to drop, and for me to realize that I will never be a good golfer. And when I realized that, I began to enjoy it, for its own sake. Maybe there's a moral for life in that, and perhaps as we get older we are given better sense to work out what really is important in life. Of course, I still try to win but that is not as important as good company, fresh air, lovely scenery and exercise. There are too many men of my age who still think they're going to be a Jack Nicklaus, and they would be far happier just being themselves! At Murvagh I'm accepted around the course and clubhouse as just another member, and not as anyone special, and I like that. Golf has helped me to relax, most of all. After Marie died I was in no mood to look at a golf course, but one day, a long time afterwards, my regular partner and I went down to see if we could still swing a club. I had my injuries from the bomb, and he had recently undergone open-heart surgery. So we set up, settled into our stance and took a swing, each in turn. To our great relief and delight we found that we could still hit a ball, maybe not well enough to win a championship, but sufficiently well to get around a course with some kind of golfing dignity, and that was a great moment. Golf has been good to me, and good for me, and I'm grateful for that. It has played a great part in my recovery, such as it is.

Another important factor has been the continuing friendship of Marie's former flatmates and colleagues Katherine, Fiona and Claire. They all trained together at the Royal Victoria Hospital and each had rooms in Bostock House, in the nurses' home. Later they moved out to hospital property nearby, and ended up by sharing a two-bedroomed flat. We got to know them all well, and called in regularly when we were in Belfast, even when Marie was not there. They were great companions and we shared in the stories and happenings which were typical of four young student nurses making their way in life.

We never underestimated the awful shock to the girls when they heard of Marie's death. One of them was in Portrush with her boyfriend when she heard the news. On the day before she died, Marie had posted a birthday card to Claire, and it arrived at her home in Belfast on the Monday morning. Her mother spotted the Enniskillen postmark, and wisely kept the letter from her, for a few days. The three girls and their parents came to the funeral, and when we met them they were shattered. It was very important to us, however, that they were there, because they had been so close to Marie.

Since her death, they have been extremely good to us. They have come together to see us, and on their own. They have been extremely faithful in putting anniversary notices in the paper and in placing flowers on Marie's grave. We have been keeping in touch with them from our end, and we have been to the wedding of two of the girls. At a time like that you think long of Marie and what might have been, but you put those kind of thoughts out of your mind and you think only of the girls and of their happiness. We hope dearly that they will still stay in touch and that they will drop in to see us, without even ringing us up in advance. Their friendship and consideration have helped to heal our wounds to some degree. We need their support more than they need ours, and that's why we always love to see them. They bring a breath of fresh air to our lives, just the way Marie did when she came breezing in for a weekend at home.

One of the reasons why we've been able to cope as a family is that we have been able to talk about Marie and her death in a normal and natural way. Some people believe that it is wrong to talk about a dead person and that this only opens old wounds. But we find it to be the opposite. It is as natural as breathing to talk about Marie, and I believe if we tried to bottle things up it would lead to all sorts of difficulties. There's not a day when Joan and I don't mention her, and we think of her many times in one day. We've now got to the stage where the family, and our friends and neighbours, can talk about her without the tears welling in our eyes.

We decided from the start not to make her bedroom into a kind of shrine, and we try to look at everything in perspective. We visit her grave regularly, and with less pain than in the past. We don't make a ritual of such visits. We've also learned to smile at the memory of Marie and at some of her antics. We don't laugh at her, but with her. I know that's what she would have wanted.

We've had tremendous support, above all, from Peter and Julie Anne. To some extent they took a back seat, right from the day of the bomb. Their support has been, and continues to be, solid and yet unobtrusive. Before the explosion they had already left home, but now they drop in almost every day, just to see that we are all right, and to tell us their news and hear ours. Peter and I work together every day in the shop, although as I get older and as I feel less fit, I am beginning to take a lower profile. Julie Anne spends time with her mother and me regularly, and she has come with us on holiday. We don't often talk about Marie in great detail, but I know that they have grieved in their own ways, and are still grieving, and that Marie is still very much with all of us. There are moments still when we are near to tears, or when we even shed a tear or two. The other night Peter and I were talking about the increasing pressures of life today, and the added pressures of Marie's tragic death, and we both ended up crying. Perhaps you could call it crying on one another's shoulders.

We also get great comfort from our grandchildren Eloise and Judith. Like any grandfather, I believe that our grandchildren are smarter and better-looking than those of anyone else! The two girls are beginning to develop their own personalities, and to an extent they are beginning to fill more and more the gap that Marie has left. We find ourselves comparing the things they do with what Marie did as a child, and this helps to ease the pain. Eloise is the more grown-up of the two, and Judith is the go-getter. People say she is like me, direct and to the point, but I think she's more like her grandmother! No matter who they're like or not like, it's great to have them near us. Without our wider family, and our friends, we would have been lost.

Even surrounded by so much love and support from family, neighbours, friends and strangers, the recovery process was long and slow. Progress would be followed by setbacks. Grief is a strange condition and I did not always understand what was going on inside me. My most disturbing setback happened one Wednesday some seven weeks after the bomb. I had settled into a routine of having an hour or so of sleep after lunch. This particular day I was alone, came downstairs and made a cup of tea while I waited for Joan to come home. I felt nothing unusual about myself, and my thoughts and actions appeared to me to be perfectly normal. Joan found me sitting in our kitchen and realized at once that I was anything but normal. Apparently I kept on asking why Marie was not at home, and why my shoulder was sore. "Had I been in an accident?" She phoned for a doctor, who had me admitted to the Erne Hospital where I stayed for four days. The Consultant confirmed that I had suffered a severe loss of memory for some ten to twelve hours, and arranged for me to go for further and exhaustive tests to the Royal Victoria Hospital in Belfast – Marie's hospital. The consensus of medical opinion was simply that the strain and pressure over the past weeks had caused the loss of memory. It was very worrying and distressing for the family, but the loss of memory disappeared. The role and support of my family was absolutely crucial at that time.

To any families who are suffering bereavement, I would say unhesitatingly, "Please accept the offers of help from your friends and neighbours. It can't be easy for them either, but they will give you the support which you will need and appreciate." When I see a news story on television about another explosion, where someone is killed or badly injured, my heart sinks, and I think to myself, "Do those poor people know what they will have to go through, and the bridges they will have to cross?" There's a temptation for everyone to say, "It won't happen to us", but it could, and it might.

The long experience has taught me that there's no purpose in being a recluse, in sitting in a corner and crying your eyes out. You have to put on a brave face and step out into the world. In nine cases out of ten, people will rally magnificently and help you. I now know what it is like to be bereaved and to try to share that experience with others, and hopefully to bring a dimension which will be helpful and relevant. In such a situation, I am reminded yet again of the rest of that quote from John Donne, which so aptly sums up the human condition:

> No man is an Island, entire of itself; every man is a piece of the Continent, a part of the main; if a clod be washed away by the sea, Europe is the less, as well as if a promontory were, as well as if a manor of thy friends or of thine own were; any man's death diminishes me, because I am involved in Mankind; And therefore never send to know for whom the bell tolls; It tolls for thee.

CHAPTER NINE

Public Eye

To some extent it was inevitable that my family and I would remain in the public eye for a long time afterwards. The original broadcasts on television and radio had been a spontaneous reaction to the death of Marie, a kind of cry from the heart. I did not know, nor could I have known, that those interviews were like pebbles thrown into a lake which would create ever-widening ripples. It was not possible to retire into anonymity, however much I would have wished to do so. But I did agree with my family's insistence that our phone number should become ex-directory. Many people were touched by what had happened. Some were shocked, others were inspired by the courage and dignity of the bereaved and injured at Enniskillen, and many, many people wrote to us expressing their thoughts and sympathy. It would have been discourteous of us to turn our backs on them and to nurse our grief in privacy.

We received sackfuls of letters, and we answered them all, as far as we could. It would have been physically impossible to answer them all personally, so we had a form of words printed and we would add a few ourselves. A friend who is head of the Commerce Department in Fermanagh College of Further Education, volunteered the help of his typing students, who sorted out our letters and typed names and addresses on hundreds of envelopes. This was a spontaneous and practical act which proved to be of great help. Indeed, I don't know how we could have dealt with our post without it. A great many of

The island town of Enniskillen. *(photo by Tom McDaniel)*

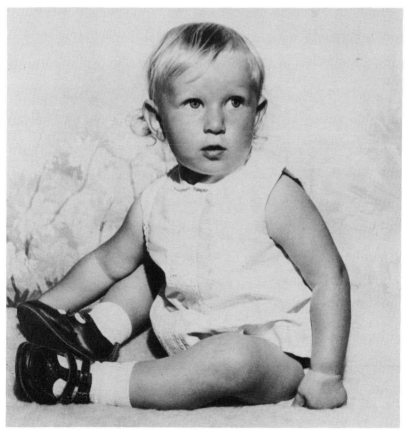

Marie, age 15 months.

Marie at the circus in Leningrad, age 6.

Marie in her last year at Primary School, age 11.

Marie, age 13, a bridesmaid at the wedding of Peter (her brother) and Ingrid. To the left are Gordon and Joan Wilson and to the right is Marie's sister, Julie Anne.

Marie at a wedding in August 1987.

Marie, with her nieces Judith (2) and Eloise (4) in October 1987.

Princess Diana talking to Joan and Gordon Wilson at a meeting with relatives of those killed by the Enniskillen bomb.

Marie on a cycling holiday in Wales, age 17.

Marie, deputy head-girl, in her final year at Enniskillen Collegiate Grammar School.

Leslie Coates, Karol Little and Marie – cup-winners at Enniskillen Feis, March 1984.

Enniskillen Collegiate Junior Singers with a cup awarded at the Belfast Musical Festival. The choir was conducted by John Henderson and accompanied by Joan. Marie is first left in the back row.

Off to guide camp in the Isle of Man. Marie is fourth from the right, back row.

Marie with her father.

the letters were moving, and some were very poignant indeed. If I were to read a number of them over again I know that I would soon be in tears.

Some were lyrically beautiful. A great many had names and addresses, and some were simply signed "Jim from Bristol" or in similar fashion. We found them helpful, but even more helpful on a second reading, because it was impossible to take in immediately the significance of what they were saying and the way that they said it. There just was not the time to sit and think, and on some occasions there were letters in the house for the best part of a week before we had time really to sit down and take them in. But I made a point of reading every letter, and on one occasion I created a bit of a row because someone had put a pile of unread letters in a box, assuming that I had seen them. Maybe it wasn't a "row" as such, but I certainly made my feelings known! People were so kind. Partly as a result of that experience I now write letters to people who have been and are suffering, and, hopefully, I now write with better understanding. Oddly, however, I find it more difficult now to express my sympathy, because I know that I can't write nearly as well as some of those who wrote to us. Some people were able to write so beautifully, and Joan and I treasure many of the things that were written and said. For example, we appreciate greatly these words from Marie McDonald, who worked with Marie in Belfast as a nursing auxiliary.

I worked with Marie Wilson in the Royal Belfast Hospital for Sick Children during the last two weeks of her life and I have never, in fifteen years as a nursing auxiliary, been so drawn to anyone.

She was the most delightful girl, with all the qualities required by a good nurse. As the days passed, I was struck by her caring and her compassion which she had in abundance. I once saw her eyes fill with tears whilst nursing a mentally handicapped child, and the gentle way she handled the sick babies was very moving.

Her spontaneous friendliness was very infectious. She greeted everyone with that lovely smile, and they responded in like manner. We had a lot of things in common, for two people of different age; we both sang in a choir, we liked the same music, she was the same age as my daughter and, another little bond, we shared the same Christian name.

On the day she was leaving our ward, I spoke to her for the last time, and my words comfort me now. I am so pleased I said them to her when she was alive and not about her when she was dead. I told her she had the most beautiful disposition and that her mother and father could be very proud of her. I also said if ever I was ill it would be lovely to be cared for by her.

As she left the ward I wished her good luck in the future. Three days later she was dead. When I saw her father on television I knew that only such a man as he could have a daughter like her.

It was my privilege to know Marie for that short time and I will never forget her. Nurse Marie Wilson was special and I am sure God thought so too.

Those words still bring tears to my eyes and afford me great comfort. They remind me of the importance of writing to someone who is in trouble or going through the "valley of the shadow". It might not seem much, at the time, but a few words of comfort can make all the difference, even from a stranger, but all the more so from an acquaintance and a friend. Letter-writing in itself is an important ministry to the bereaved and to the ill and their families.

Another source of love and sympathy was provided by flowers. They came in bouquets, baskets and pots. Joan, who knows about these things, was especially appreciative. They were sent by folk known and unknown to us, and some asked that the flowers should be placed on Marie's grave. Indeed, from time to time, even three years later, we receive cheques to buy flowers in Marie's memory, and we regularly find fresh flowers on her grave, and don't know who placed them there.

Such anonymous care and concern was, and is, very much appreciated. We also appreciated, in contrast, the messages and in some cases the visits from well-known people. For example, the Duke of Edinburgh sent us a letter of personal sympathy and condolence, mentioning the fact that Marie had been a holder of his Gold Award. The Prime Minister Mrs Thatcher sent me a lovely personal note when the news broke that I had been in hospital with loss of memory. She had come to Enniskillen earlier to take part in a rearranged Remembrance Day Service.

The original parade and service did not take place because of the bomb. Mrs Thatcher's presence in Enniskillen was appreciated by all of us, especially as she had taken some trouble to rearrange her hectic schedule. After the service she had to rush off, literally, on Government business and we did not have time to meet her personally.

It's surprising how a visit or a few words from someone representing the whole country can have an effect. The visit of the Prince and Princess of Wales to Enniskillen was a good example of this. About nine days after the bombing I was in bed, and still feeling the effects of it all, when a policewoman called. She said, "We're expecting VIPs to come to Enniskillen, and I'm not sure who, but we would like you and your family to be at the police station by 10.00 a.m." She also said something which stuck in my memory. She asked for "Blood relatives only!"

We arrived at the police station and from there we were taken to an army base at the small airport at St Angelo, just outside Enniskillen. On the way the police said, "We think that the Prince and Princess of Wales are coming but we're not sure". By the time we arrived at the reception area it was confirmed that the Royal couple had in fact landed. They had gone by car to the Erne Hospital to meet some of the injured, and then they were scheduled to come back to the airport and to meet a number of relatives. The organizers of the visit explained that the royal couple wished to talk to all the relatives present, away from the public gaze. Television and newspaper cameramen would be allowed one minute only, at the beginning, and would then be moved out of the room. We were asked whether we, the Wilson family, would meet the Prince and Princess for the cameras, so that the news people would get their pictures, and then go? Not for the first time, and certainly not for the last, I felt I was being projected as the "Face" of Enniskillen to those outside it, and was somewhat ill-at-ease about the role I was being asked to play. I had no brief to speak for others who had been tragically bereaved. Indeed, I found it difficult, to say the least, to deal with our own situation. But I wished to be as helpful as possible to everyone, in the circumstances.

We were ushered into a room, and eventually Prince Charles

came in with the Princess of Wales slightly behind him. We were at the head of the line. The Prince shook my hand and moved straight away to Joan in order not to keep the Princess standing there with, as we say in Ulster, "One arm as long as the other". She at once moved forward to speak to me, and so was 'stuck' with me until Prince Charles moved on. There was nowhere else for her to go! Later on Joan told me that she had been very impressed by Prince Charles. She remarked on his great depth of feeling; he had spoken to her most sympathetically. She felt that he was a sincere man, and very likable. She had also been struck by his "beautiful eyes" as she called them!

Princess Diana is even prettier than she looks from her photographs. She really is a lovely girl, and easy to talk to. That morning we had received, by special post, a present from her mother, and when I told her she already knew about it. This was a good conversation piece, because in such a situation it was not just easy at first to find the right words to say. No doubt the royal couple were nervous too. People don't always realize that "public figures" can be nervous just like anybody else. The Prince and Princess were coming to a situation of great sensitivity just a few days after the bomb. I think it was the first time they had met a group of relatives whose lives had been devastated on such a scale. So it can't have been easy for them either. But they both coped very well, and their visit was a great lift for all of us. Our daughter Julie Anne was just thrilled to meet them. Enniskillen as a whole was feeling low, and the royal couple gave the town a great boost. We felt that it was a very fine gesture on their part.

The attendant publicity meant, however, that we were still in the public eye. Some weeks later I was phoned by a reporter from one of the tabloid newspapers in London. He said to me, "Have you heard that you are going to be mentioned in the Queen's Christmas Broadcast? We've been told that she's going to mention Northern Ireland and that she will mention reconciliation and toleration. Have you any comment?" This was the first time I had heard of it, and, somewhat bewildered by it all, I indicated that I had nothing to say. Later I learned of the furore which occurred in London when details of Her

Majesty's message had been disclosed, without permission, long before the broadcast.

Then, on Christmas Eve, Her Majesty's Lieutenant for County Fermanagh called with me and told me that Her Majesty proposed to mention me in her Christmas Message. I thanked him for the information, and I felt that this was the greatest recognition possible, that all of us in Enniskillen should be remembered by the Queen in her broadcast which went out to the whole world.

Naturally we listened on Christmas Day, and she indeed mentioned Enniskillen. I felt that if the Queen had thought it worthwhile to mention our family by name she must have been moved personally by what had been said in Enniskillen after the bombing. She noted that the strength of our family came from our Christian conviction and she went on:

> All of us will echo their prayer that out of the personal tragedies of Enniskillen may come a reconciliation between the communities. She also said, It is only too easy for passionate loyalty to one's own country, race or religion, or even to one's favourite football club, to be corroded into intolerance, bigotry and ultimately into violence. We have witnessed some frightening examples of this in recent years. All too often, intolerance creates the resentment and anger which fill the headlines and divide communities and nations and even families.
>
> Of course, it is right that people should hold their beliefs and their faiths strongly and sincerely, but perhaps we should also have the humility to accept that, while we each have a right to our own convictions, others have a right to theirs too. I am afraid that the Christmas message of goodwill has usually evaporated by the time Boxing Day is over. This year I hope we will continue to remember the many innocent victims of violence and intolerance and the suffering of their families. Christians are taught to love their neighbours, not just at Christmas, but all the year round. I hope we will all help each other to have a Happy Christmas and, when the New Year comes, resolve to work for tolerance and understanding between the people.

It was a fine address, and I was greatly moved by what she had to say, and the way that she said it. But then I was also greatly

moved a few days later when I was walking along a corridor
at the Royal Victoria Hospital. A wee "tea-lady" recognized me,
and left her trolley. She rushed across and said, "God Bless you
and thank you, and I'm sorry for your trouble". I found that very
affecting in just the same way. Sincerely expressed sympathy has
no boundaries and no barriers, whether it's from the Queen
herself or a tea-lady in the Royal Victoria Hospital. It comes
from the heart, and it goes to the heart. Sympathy from the
famous is given a bit more media coverage, but deep down it's
exactly the same emotion, and precious in itself.

Around that time also I got caught up in the whole business of
awards and nominations for "Man of the Year". It was something
which was very well meant, but not to be taken too personally.
It was a profound and public sentiment for Enniskillen and for
all that had taken place there. Not long after the explosion,
I was voted as "Man of the Year" in a BBC Radio Four poll,
ahead of Mr Gorbachev and Prince Charles! Of course I was
grateful for BBC listeners to think of me in such a way, but in
my heart of hearts I knew I could not be compared with such
men. They were on the world's stage and I was just the man from
Enniskillen. Others had suffered as much as I had, and I was a
bit uncomfortable about this kind of media attention, however
well meant. On the other hand, I was aware that if someone was
giving an award or an accolade it would have been churlish to
refuse or to renounce such a thing, because such awards and
accolades were a genuine expression of sympathy, not only for
me but for all those people caught up in the Enniskillen tragedy.
So I did my best to accept all the awards as gracefully as possible,
and to fit in with the wishes of the organizers, all the while
thinking that it was on behalf of many others also that I was
receiving so much attention.

Some of these events, of course, were more high-powered
than others. At the Dorchester Hotel, London, I accepted a
posthumous award to Marie for bravery. She was remembered
as a "Woman of Courage" in the 1987 Women of Achievement
Awards presented by Batchelors Foods and the readers of
Woman's Own. Other winners included Kate Adie, the television
news reporter; Fatima Whitbread, the athlete; Catherine Cook-

son, the novelist; Esther Rantzen, the television presenter; and Mrs Raisa Gorbachev, who was named as International Woman of the Year. Her award was received by a representative of the Soviet Embassy in London. All in all, it was an impressive ceremony, and I felt a little bit out of my depth at first. It was all a long way from the Main Street in Manorhamilton! At the Dorchester I sat beside Esther Rantzen, who talked to me at length about Enniskillen and about Marie. When it was my turn to collect Marie's award, the whole audience gave a standing ovation, and this took me by surprise, just in the same way that I had been surprised by the applause in the Roman Catholic church in Enniskillen just a few days after the bombing. It seemed that wherever we went, people remembered and recognized the suffering of Enniskillen, and that was very moving.

There were several other awards, including the title "Man of the Year" from the Royal Association for Disability and Rehabilitation (RADAR) who also honoured Sir John Mills, the actor; P.C. Richard Coombes of Enfield, Middlesex, for protecting colleagues during the Broadwater Farm riots and his courage in overcoming his injuries; Brian Cleaver from the West Midlands who became the first man to complete the London Marathon on crutches; Alun Thomas of Cardiff who climbed a hundred-foot cliff to save ten people trapped by the tide; members of Dover Lifeboat who led the rescue of three men washed overboard; Philip Scott from Hampshire who was paralysed after a motor-cycle accident but later built a plane for the disabled; and Captain Soubhi Yousseff of Kuwaiti Airlines for his courage during the hi-jack of his airliner. When you consider the distinction and personal courage of all these people, I was honoured to be listed in their company.

There were also awards given by people in Ireland, and this was particularly important to me because I was very conscious of the impact of Enniskillen on Ireland as a whole. I was honoured to receive one of the 1988 "People of the Year" Awards. These were organized by the Rehabilitation Institute, and one of the most popular awards of the night went to big Jack Charlton, the manager of the Irish Republic's soccer team, who had restored such pride to Irish football and later brought the Irish team to the World Cup Finals. He was a real hero! I was also delighted to share in the occasion with Mrs Carmencita Hederman, the then former Lord Mayor of Dublin who had done such capital work for her city. She had come to Enniskillen as Lord Mayor and had shown moving and heartfelt sympathy and deep humanity. Her actions had spoken volumes. On the Awards night in Dublin, the then Minister for Commerce, Mr Ray Burke, had referred to what I had said on television and radio, and added that these words of "compassion" had been heard throughout the world. He also said, "I feel sure that these words helped to change any possible thoughts of retaliatory violence into, instead, a renewed commitment to peace, reconciliation and dialogue, for this man represents above all, the voice of peace and dialogue."

These were very big sentiments to apply to me and I felt that, in a way, I was carrying something much greater than anything I had envisaged when I had spoken initially on television and radio. It was as if people, all over the world, were expecting more of "Gordon Wilson" than the real Gordon Wilson himself, and yet deep down I knew what they were all trying to say. Peace and dialogue are indivisible, they are concepts of purity, they cannot be bettered. They are light in darkness, they are the eternal good battling with evil, they hold the key to the future of the world. And here was I listening to these words and collecting awards and honours not for myself but for something way beyond me, for the very nobility of life at the best that it can be. Or so it seemed to me. And that was something which did not settle on my shoulders easily, but I understood what it meant, what people were trying to say and to convey. In a way it was so very beautiful, in the midst of all the horror and suffering and tragedy and loss, like the "terrible beauty" of the Irish poet, W.B. Yeats. So I did my best to meet people where they were, with their thoughts and sympathy and awards expressed in their own way, knowing that it was all part of a greater whole which in some way, some day, would contribute to a greater peace in our own land.

A peace group from Tipperary presented their award in a simple yet moving ceremony. A television crew from Radio

Telefis Eireann, the Dublin-based television station, covered the event, and their reporter asked me to make a comment on something political which had happened that day. He said to me privately that as a professional he had to ask me that kind of question, but I also made the point that I did not want to be drawn into a political or religious controversy which would detract from anything which had been said or done in Enniskillen. The reporter told his boss. My views were taken into account, and they did not take the "political" angle. But it underlined the constant problem of dealing with the media, on the one hand not wanting to be rude or unhelpful but on the other not wanting to be encouraged to move into areas where I would be quickly out of my depth. And yet there was an obligation to be co-operative with those who were honouring not only me but Enniskillen as well.

A good example of this was "Wogan" on BBC Television. One morning I had a phone call from the producer. "Would you appear on the show?", he asked. I agreed, even though I felt that this was "big league" for me. Television forces you to play a somewhat different role. You do not feel your normal self with all those cameras trained on you. It's a major step from working behind a counter in a draper's shop in Enniskillen to appearing "live" on television before a national audience. I always try to take things as they come and do the decent thing, but the Wogan Show was a bad experience. I had reservations from the start, because I did not see this as my type of programme, in the sense that it did not normally deal with my type of situation. I saw it as entertainment, chatty and light, and I wasn't the man to be chatty or light to provide entertainment.

This was not the fault of Terry Wogan. It just was not my scene, and I came away from the programme feeling "That was a nothing". The RADAR Awards people had encouraged me to appear, for a little advance publicity, and this seemed to make sense. I felt therefore that I would be letting them down if I did not do it. You join a band and you have to play with the band, or to put it another way, you become a member of a club and you abide by the rules. So I came away from the Wogan show feeling that I had said little and that I had not said it very well. Perhaps this was due to my nerves which took over, and the uncertainty in my own mind. However much I rehearsed, the setting seemed contrived, and the fact that it was "live" was also a pressure. Other guests that evening included a "way out" musical group, and I did not feel really at home. There is also the reality that live television is all over in five or six minutes, and you don't have the atmosphere of, say, a dinner engagement where you can acclimatize yourself to the surroundings before you are asked to speak.

I liked Terry Wogan as a person. He's a professional and he's sound, friendly and helpful. Perhaps he was a little nervous too, because this was very much a one-off. Maybe he was not sure of what I wanted or what I would like to say. But from my point of view it simply did not work. It was all wrong. And as a result I became very wary of all sorts of programmes, and turned down many offers for discussions and documentaries, from North and South of the Border, and across the water. I also turned down a request to appear on an Esther Rantzen programme. She had a series of half-hour interviews and was kind enough to ask me if I would be one of six people to be questioned, each for a half-hour programme. I did not want to see myself talking on television for half an hour. I was anxious not to overstate my case or to suggest that I had a mission to fulfil, or to end up by saying the wrong thing. A good friend had told me, on the day after the bomb went off, "Be careful about what you say on the media. Keep it simple, and try to use the kind of language which ordinary people will understand." Therefore I had a reluctance to become involved in the kind of programme where very quickly I might be at sea, in terms of religion and politics. As a result, my appearances on the media have been very limited because I want to keep a certain degree of privacy. Not long ago, again in the Royal Victoria Hospital, I met someone who obviously knew me but who couldn't place my face. And that cheered me a great deal. Maybe in a few years' time I will be forgotten completely, but Enniskillen will be remembered long after me; and that's how it should be.

People might wonder why I'm producing a book, and I thought hard before taking it on. But I decided to put my thoughts on paper, partly because it's easier to choose my words this way. There is not the same pressure from the clock or from a television studio floor manager. I can choose or discard words, yet still talk from the heart. In a way it's a different kind of pressure but it's something I can live with. I've had time to look back, to reap the benefit of hindsight, and I can get a more settled and objective view. It is also important to share with other people who have been bereaved. Everyone has his or her cross to bear, and it's a great help to identify with those who have been through a similar experience. At least we are not on our own. Joan and I found a special comfort from the letters and messages of those who had been through their own gruelling experiences. It may be that someone, somewhere, will find a little comfort from what I have to say and to share. But most of all, I would like to think of this book as a voice for Marie. She is at the heart of the story and yet she is unable to speak for herself. So I hope that something of Marie, the person, also comes through. She was, and still is, very precious to her family, and she can speak only through us and through our memories of her.

The other day I was sorting through old papers and found a scribbled note of Marie's which was written just a year before she died. It was during her time at the Royal Victoria Hospital, and she was wrestling with many doubts, as we all do from time to time whatever the state of our faith. It is a very beautiful glimpse of the Marie we all loved, and still love, to this day. She called it "My prayer, after studying the Epistle of James, Book 7".

Thank you Lord, for your Word. Without you I, too, would be an orphan. Lord help me by bringing others to be blessed, also help me to grow in maturity and completeness, and receive the crown of life. Lord, my career is up-front in my mind at the moment, with Night Duty. Help me to listen to my patients and act on their problems. Lord, I pray for my great friends Mum and Dad, thank you for their love . . . "Jaws" [her sister] please Lord be with her, and especially Anne-Marie. I pray for Northern Ireland and the whole world. I pray for the church that I may do my role. Thank you Lord. Give me wisdom.

That was also the voice of Marie which I would like people to remember when they think of Enniskillen.

CHAPTER TEN

Forgiveness

After I made my television and radio broadcast on the night of Marie's death, some people said, "He must have been drugged, or sedated or deeply shocked to have said such a thing! He could not possibly mean that he bore no ill-will towards the bombers." They believed that no rational man could have said what I said. On the other extreme I was misquoted to such an extent that many people read far more into what I said than actually was the case. I did not mention the word "forgiveness", though many people believed that I had "forgiven" the bombers who had killed Marie and the others, and had left so many families in a state of devastation.

On the whole, however, I got a good press. What I had said seemed to strike a chord, and people were loving, supportive and helpful. This helped Joan and me to pull through. Such support came not only from friends and family, and the people of Enniskillen and of Ireland North and South, but from Britain, and all over the world. We were conscious of being sustained by a solid wall of support which seemed to surround us like a great shield of protection. The great majority of people approved of what I had said and done, and those who criticized me were in a small minority. Some things were said which hurt me, especially from those who claimed that I was speaking in a kind of dream. There were a number of very hurtful phone calls, including one from a woman who asked me bitterly, "When you are going to stop dancing on your daughter's grave?"

Different people reacted in different ways. Some told me later that they did not come into my shop because they were not sure what to say. They were not unsympathetic, but they were not sure how to put their feelings in words. Many people are like that, and they feel inadequate because they are not able to express their feelings in a way which they would wish to. And others said simply, "That man and his wife need a bit of peace, after all they've been through". I still meet those who say, "I haven't seen you since your 'Trouble', how are you?" Maybe it's nothing more than that, but it's their way of saying, "I'm sorry; I am thinking about you". And as time goes on it is easier for other people to come to terms with what happened.

Over the months following the bomb there were all sorts of responses. I had letters of invitation to join the Muslim faith, the Jewish faith and all kind of other faiths. Maybe they thought it would do me good, but it was all a bit much for a dyed-in-the-wool Methodist like me! Perhaps the most bizarre invitation of all came from a man in New York. He was some kind of theatrical agent who wanted me to appear on a lecture tour in America and Canada. He made the contact with me through a mutual friend, and I was assured that the agent was perfectly serious. His words to my friend were, "Does this guy Wilson realize he is sitting on a million bucks?" It didn't take me long to decide to decline this offer!

In most cases I believe that the people who talked to me, and who still walk over to meet me, are sincere, although there is sometimes the person about whom, initially, you have doubts. It may be just their choice of words. And then I think about it again, and I come to the conclusion that they are a hundred per cent straight and sincere. I often think that I'm far too sensitive about what people say or don't say.

I am always particularly impressed and much encouraged when I listen to people who have suffered a tragedy in their own family. It helps me enormously to learn how they are coping. I feel that I know something of the load that they are bearing and am very often moved to tears as I hear them speak of their personal experiences. No two experiences are alike in every respect, but while the shock and the grief and hurt are always apparent, people are dealing with their anguish in different ways. It seems to me that there is no one common formula, and that every case is handled individually. This has proved to be the case even amongst members of my family.

There are still the bad days for me, even when I think that I have made progress. To be honest, there are days in public when I'm feeling low, and maybe someone comes across to me to say a few words and to express his or her condolences, and I find myself going through the motions. But deep down I'm saying, "God forgive me, but why can't they leave me in peace?" It's only a thought, and it goes away quickly. I would hate people not to come across because they are afraid of disturbing me. Such words are usually a comfort, but I can't be one hundred per cent receptive all the time. I'm only human, and, as I've written elsewhere, some people expect more of "Gordon Wilson" than the real Gordon Wilson himself.

I like to think that it was the real Gordon Wilson who spoke to the BBC's reporter, Mike Gaston, on the evening of the bomb, when I said ". . . I have lost my daughter, and we shall miss her. But I bear no ill-will. I bear no grudge. Dirty sort of talk is not going to bring her back. . . . She was a pet. She's dead. She's in heaven and we'll meet again. Don't ask me please, for a purpose. I don't have a purpose. I don't have an answer. But I know there has to be a plan. If I didn't think that, I would commit suicide. It's part of a greater plan, and God is good. And we shall meet again."

I did not use the word "forgive" in that broadcast, nor in any later one, but people understood that my words were about forgiveness. Our Lord taught us to pray, "Forgive us our sins, as we forgive those who sin against us". We ask God to forgive us, but we are always subjected to his condition that we must forgive others. God's forgiveness is ultimate, ours is the forgiveness of man to man. To me, the two become one. It's as simple and yet as profound as that. My words were not intended as a statement of theology or of righteousness, rather they were from the heart, and they expressed exactly how I felt at the time, and as I still do. Countless sermons have been preached on the subject of forgiveness and many books written. I do not pretend to understand all of them, since they sometimes seem to be contradictory. I prefer my conception of the simple, uncomplicated, and yet so demanding words of Christ in the Lord's Prayer.

If, for example, someone breaks a valuable vase in my home and they say, "Please forgive me", this is easy to do on a human scale; but when you talk about Enniskillen you are touching on a vast subject that exceeds the limits of our humanity. Eleven people died in the tragedy. They cannot be brought back and they were all human beings, made like all of us in the image of God. Those who have to account for this deed will have to face a judgement of God which is way beyond the forgiveness of Gordon Wilson. More than once I have made this point and the press have produced headlines suggesting that Gordon Wilson is unforgiving, which I'm not. I do not regard myself as unforgiving in the commonly-accepted sense of that term. On the contrary, I hope that I am a man of a forgiving nature. Human beings may be, can be, and indeed ought to be, able to forgive on human terms, but ultimately it is for God to forgive, and on his terms.

When I think directly of the people responsible for killing Marie and the others, I don't bear them nasty thoughts. I am certainly not lying in my bed at night worrying about them. As human beings they have their own pieces to pick up, and it's not for me to go out of my way to think ill of them or to bear them a grudge. They will ultimately have to face their God, as I will. The fact that I don't bear them any malice might be partly a protection on my own part. It would be extremely stressful for me if I were to spend a lot of time thinking of recrimination or about ways of trying to "get back" at these people. Therefore, a part of me is trying to push it all away for fear of being hurt even more. Joan, as a contrast, has said to me that she would want to meet them face to face and simply ask them, "Why? Why did you do this? How can you hurt other human beings so? What is your justification for such acts, if you have any at all?" I know that Joan still prays for the bombers every day, that they will seek God's forgiveness and think about what they are doing.

For my part I have no desire to meet these people, and as far as I am concerned it would serve no purpose. There is nothing

I can say or do on this side of the grave which will bring Marie back. And yet I believe in the rule of law, and if I had to go through a court case I would have to comply with the law, to do my duty. It would be wrong for me to give any impression that gunmen and bombers should be allowed to walk the streets freely. But whether or not they are judged here on earth by a court of law, I have no doubt they will have to face their final judgement before Almighty God, and that this will be a lonely judgement. The laws of the land are manmade, but the ultimate law lies with God.

Nevertheless, I still pray for the bombers, and I continue to bear them no ill-will. Better men than I have wrestled with the whole concept of forgiveness and have failed. I believe that I do my very best in human terms to show forgiveness, but the last word rests with God and that those who seek his forgiveness will need to repent. At that level, such a judgement is way beyond me. All I can do is to continue not to think evil or malicious thoughts about these people and to go on bearing them no ill-will. I wasn't angry at the time, and I'm not angry now.

At no time did I want to go and "get" anyone, never mind "kill" anybody. I accepted that what happened was part of a greater plan. I still believe that. Marie is where I believe she is, in heaven. I don't think that I could have accepted or lived with the reality of a twenty-year-old girl sitting helplessly in a wheelchair, paralysed from the waist down and with brain damage. Marie was terribly injured by the explosion, and if she had lived she might have been left like that. That's something I think about, and perhaps I'm only comforting myself, but I believe that she is better off where she is now than lying in a coma day after day after day. People have said to me, "Gordon, you are very brave", but if you want to see real bravery, you should look at the face of Noreen Hill whose husband Ronnie was injured in the bomb and has been in a coma ever since. That's real courage, as far as I'm concerned.

For my part I want to go on with my life, doing my best to pick up the pieces, like all others. The bombers who caused such terrible suffering and loss will have to try to pick up their own pieces, no matter how many there are, and how difficult they are to pick up. It cannot be easy knowing that, directly or indirectly, you are responsible for the deaths of so many people and for the maiming of so many others, and for the suffering and despair of the relatives. It cannot be easy to look at yourself in the mirror, in such a situation. But I'm not going to add to the hatreds by talking about bitterness or revenge. I'll go on praying for all of them, and leave the rest to God. That's the only way I can handle it, and still live with myself.

CHAPTER ELEVEN

The Spirit of Enniskillen

People sometimes ask me, "Can you see any good coming out of the evil which caused the deaths and injuries in Enniskillen?" That's a very big question, and there are no glib or easy answers. How can good come out of the evil that caused the deaths of eleven people and the maiming of so many others? How can good come from the violence in Northern Ireland which has caused so many deaths and injuries, and such tragedy and heartbreak? Any man or woman who attempts to give simple answers is on perilous ground.

I never cease to think about the bomb and its aftermath, especially as the Troubles go on and on. Every new incident brings the Enniskillen bombing back to mind, and each time it affects me, especially if it is local. A short time ago Joan and I were about half a mile away from a bomb which went off in another part of Fermanagh. That shook both of us. I'm still nervous, in general, and when I go to Belfast I'm very conscious of bomb scares and roadblocks and traffic diversions caused by bomb warnings. Certainly I have more fears than before, and it's difficult to explain, unless you've been through the trauma of an explosion. Perhaps "explain" is the wrong word. It's just that I now know more about the risks to life and limb, and what it will entail in human terms and in suffering for those individuals and their families and friends who are directly caught up in a bomb. And there's always the fear that I might be a victim again.

Looking back, I still count myself very lucky to be alive and to have come through as well as I have in physical terms. At least six of the people who died in Enniskillen were within three paces of where I stood. I don't know why I escaped. The people beside me were killed by falling masonry, and those across the street were killed by the bomb blast. I read somewhere about the scientific details of a bomb, and these are frightening. Apparently there's a shock wave which travels at some thirteen thousand miles per hour. This slows down quickly and does not create the greatest damage, though human skin and bone close to the bomb can be severely affected. The major damage is caused by a blast wave which follows at some six hundred miles per hour. It has the pressure of pent-up gases behind it, and the blast wave has a tearing, heaving, wrecking motion. Associated with the blast wave is a fireball which lasts for micro-seconds, and the combination of shock wave, blast and fireball can be devastating. It's not good to dwell on such things. I don't brood, but I reflect a lot, especially when I hear or read about bombs going off elsewhere.

When I think of what happened at Enniskillen I don't begin even to pretend to understand why such an awful tragedy should have occurred. As St Paul writes in his First Epistle to the Corinthians, "For now we see through a glass, darkly". We have to continue living with the reality and the aftermath of Enniskillen, even though we don't understand why or how it could be part of a greater plan, but we will understand, some day.

When people ask about the possibility of good coming out of the evil of the Enniskillen bombing, I try to redefine the terms. It is not so much that good as such can come out of pure evil, but rather, in the case of Enniskillen and elsewhere, that love can and will triumph over hatred. Some people might think I'm merely whistling in the dark, but I believe deeply in the power of love. One of my favourite readings is the famous "Desiderata":

Many persons strive for high ideals; and everywhere life is full of heroism. . . . Neither be cynical about love; for in the face of all aridity and disenchantment it is perennial as the grass.

Therefore when I think about and reflect upon the aftermath of Enniskillen I am taking the wide view that love can, does and will triumph over hatred. In a general sense the good that came out of Enniskillen is partly that no "bad" came as a result, that hatred was not allowed to triumph. Relationships could have been soured, in that some people believed that the bomb was aimed deliberately at the Protestant community; but on the contrary, the bomb and its aftermath brought people together in a quite remarkable way. Enniskillen, because of its roughly equal mixture of Protestants and Roman Catholics, has good relationships, and these were maintained and fostered after the bomb, in community and personal ways. There were the church services and public expressions of grief, and there were countless little messages of sympathy and support from people in both communities.

The Roman Catholic community, right from the top to the man in the street, were altogether sympathetic and showed this concern for me both privately and in corporate acts of support, kindness and commiseration. This was something I appreciated very much. For example, the Mayor of Limerick came to Marie's funeral in his civic robes and to express personally his condolences and those of the people of Limerick. He did not have to come so far to do that, but I appreciated his gesture.

Within the Protestant community the immediate reaction was that of grief and sorrow, as well as shock and abhorrence that such a thing could have happened. But, significantly, there were no words about retribution. There was anger, hurt, questioning, but no mention about reprisal. One of the good things about the Enniskillen aftermath was the lack of any Protestant "backlash". I never heard a word about that, at the time or since, and I am most thankful that no one else suffered as a direct result of our own suffering and loss.

It is important to make the point that the enormity of the bomb only sank in slowly to us, and by degrees. It was a matter of days rather than hours before we began to put together all the pieces. In the first few days there were the many practicalities of the funerals and one's personal injuries, and of meeting people. There wasn't even time to grieve privately. The only place where I could grieve was in my own bed at night, and then the next morning it was time to meet more people and to face up to more situations. I have made the point several times, and I can't make it often enough, that we found the prayer-support very helpful. As a family we were conscious of a deep undercurrent of prayer from countless unseen people which helped us tremendously. I had always believed in prayer, but I've never been so conscious of the sheer power of prayer as in that week. It showed what other people can do for others, and I commend that to everyone who feels they want to help but maybe cannot do so in a direct way. Your prayers for others in trouble can, and do, make all the difference.

In a practical sense another of the good things to come from Enniskillen was the Appeal Fund which was set up shortly afterwards. It was initially the idea of Gerry Burns, the Clerk and Chief Executive of Fermanagh District Council. He received a flood of phone calls from people offering assistance and asking how they might help, so it seemed to him that an Enniskillen Appeal Fund would provide an opportunity for many people to show their sympathy and solidarity in a practical way. A panel of Trustees was set up, representing the four main churches and the two main political groups in the area. The money flooded in, although the main objective of the Fund was not just financial. Gerry Burns and the others were aware that many people outside Enniskillen wanted to identify with the hurt and the pain of our community, and that the Fund would provide an opportunity to do this in a tangible way. The response was overwhelming, and donations came from all parts of the world. There were gifts from places as far apart as Pakistan and Vancouver, and from all areas of Europe and the United Kingdom.

The response, financial and otherwise, from the Irish Republic was extremely heart-warming. Almost every town and village sent its book of condolences, in many cases brought personally by a representative, and in all there were about three hundred thousand signatures from the Irish Republic alone. Gerry Burns tells the story of one small village in the West of Ireland which sent two representatives to Enniskillen, one Protestant and one Roman Catholic, bearing its book of condolences. They also brought a large salmon to demonstrate another kind of practical support, and this was duly taken to the Erne Hospital and shared among many of those who had been so actively involved during the aftermath of the bomb. A number of donations came from Fermanagh people in various parts of the world, and altogether it was a most inspiring exercise. They raised about £660,000, and eighty per cent of this was given to the families of the bereaved and to the injured.

The organizers had reviewed the arrangements made after other disasters, including Bradford, when a large number of people had been killed and injured during a fire in a soccer stadium. In Enniskillen they set up a panel to advise on claims. This consisted of a surgeon, a psychiatrist and a businessman. A social worker helped to present the claims, and the Trustees made the final decisions in the light of the advice from the special panel of experts. The Trustees also decided that money would be set aside for a permanent memorial, and also for the establishment of an Enniskillen Youth and Community Trust. This Trust provides a means whereby people from both communities can support events and projects to assist the elderly, the sick and the lonely. So, in all these ways, the Enniskillen Appeal Fund demonstrated the good that is in the Enniskillen community and in people everywhere. This support, financial and otherwise, has provided tangible help to the bereaved and their families, and also made provision for a memorial to the others, as well as a living memorial of co-operation with both communities. As such, I found the entire project most heartening, and in its own way, humbling. It's amazing how much people care when you touch their hearts.

Another important development was the Fund organized by the *Daily Mirror* newspaper. It was the brain-child of Mary Riddell, a feature writer on the paper, and it became known as the Marie Wilson Memorial Fund. The idea was to send money to the Royal Victoria Hospital where Marie had been a nurse, and they raised £35,000 from people all over the British Isles. There were very few big donations – the *Mirror* is not read by many industrial tycoons! – but there were a great many small donations, and the total was magnificent. It showed how much people really cared.

The money from the Fund was used in various ways – about £5,000 was sent to the Royal College of Nursing, and £2,500 was donated to the Erne Hospital. Some of the proceeds were used in the Royal Victoria Hospital to furnish a room specially kept for the relatives of seriously ill patients. This was called the Livingstone Room in memory of a well-known surgeon in the hospital, and we gave a painting in memory of Marie. The artist, Marie Prenter, who is the wife of my golf partner, sent another of her own paintings for the room. The balance was kept to help fund research scholarships for nurses. We were grateful that Marie's memory was perpetuated and that the money was given to causes which, I am sure, would have been close to her heart. It was also good to come to know Mary Riddell as a friend, and we still stay in touch.

Another excellent project arising out of the Enniskillen tragedy had an important international dimension. On the day of the bombing, Mr Roy McMurtry, the then Canadian High Commissioner in London, was staying with Mr Tom King, the then Secretary of State for Northern Ireland, at his official residence in Hillsborough Castle. Mr McMurtry felt moved to persuade his Government later on to do something about Enniskillen, and he helped to set up a scheme called the Marie Wilson Voyage of Hope, whereby a small number of young Protestants and Roman Catholics went to Canada in 1988 for a three-week visit. This was not a holiday, but rather an opportunity to find out how people in other parts of the world handle their problems. Stephen Ross, who was injured in the bomb, was one of the participants, and he confirmed to me the value of such a scheme. It enabled our young people to find out more about each other and to bring back a wider vision of the outside world. In the first year they worked in Ontario, and under the supervision of doctors and nurses they took part in the day-to-day running of a camp for handicapped young people.

Their presence in Canada also provided an opportunity for their hosts to see the kinder face of Northern Ireland, and they were able to make the point that there was also good news in their native Province. That was good for everyone concerned, and it was a most practical way for our Canadian friends to show their sympathy and respect. The young people who were selected all came from the County of Fermanagh, and they had a get-together before they went to Canada. There was, naturally, a certain nervousness and unfamiliarity because they had not met before, and there were young people from both communities who had had little opportunity to reach across the divide. After they returned to Northern Ireland I noticed that they had an assuredness which was very obvious. A new dimension had been added to their lives, and they were able to talk very easily of their experiences. The three weeks in Canada had made an unbelievable difference to them.

The scheme has been in existence for three years and I hope that the Canadian Government will continue to back it. Apart from any connection with Marie Wilson, it is worth sustaining in itself because it allows Fermanagh young people to gain an wider perspective on life and to learn more about themselves and one another. In this way they will bring back a little more enlightenment to their own communities. It's a project of which Marie would have approved, and it's the sort of thing which she would have loved to have been on herself.

Yet another project which is helping to broaden the horizons of young people is the "Spirit of Enniskillen" Bursaries. These were started by Dr Brian Mawhinney, the Government Minister in charge of Education in Northern Ireland. Ten days after the bomb he was sufficiently moved to come and see me at my home, although his visit was totally unexpected. One evening I had a phonecall from a civil servant informing me that the Minister was at a local hotel, and asking whether or not I would be happy to see him. I immediately agreed, and shortly afterwards he arrived at my home, complete with police cars and bodyguards! This somewhat bemused my bank manager, who later arrived to deal with some business we had in common and wondered what on earth was going on. Dr Mawhinney spoke very sincerely and sympathetically, but at that stage there was no mention whatever of any government initiative. Some time later, however, we saw Dr Mawhinney at Stormont and he outlined his project. He suggested that it might be called the Marie Wilson Bursary Fund or indeed the Gordon Wilson Bursary Fund, but I was not happy with either suggestion. Finally we settled for the "Spirit of Enniskillen" Bursaries. The idea is to encourage young people in the sixteen to nineteen age range to travel outside Northern Ireland and, on their return, to use their experience to help foster bridge-building at home. The scheme is somewhat different to the Canadian model, in that there are several destinations, rather than one specific place. However the broad thrust is the same, mainly to allow young people to see other societies and hopefully to bring something back.

The "Spirit of Enniskillen" Bursaries are aimed particularly at bringing young people to areas where others have been, and are, coping with community problems, in the hope that they will relate to the community problems back home. The scheme was admirably summarized by Dr Mawhinney at a reception in Hillsborough Castle for thirty-one Protestant and Catholic teenagers who won the first Bursaries. He said:

> I was delighted with the response to the award scheme, which I launched following the Remembrance Day bombing in Enniskillen in 1987. It shows that there is a growing reservoir of goodwill in the Province and that many people from all sections of the community are prepared to learn about and respect the other person's point of view. Of course, there are different attitudes and aspirations in Northern Ireland society and these will continue to exist. Nevertheless, it must always be remembered that difference does not necessarily mean division. There are great strengths in our diverse cultural heritage and we should always endeavour to build on what we have in common, rather than dwell on what divides us.
>
> These bursaries are enabling the young people to travel abroad and see at first hand how other communities have resolved their conflicts. This process of self-education is one way of helping people to overcome their historical prejudices and hopefully they will return to their own communities and play their part in helping

to bridge divisions and promote better community understanding and tolerance.

The Government originally provided £150,000 to start the scheme, with the proceeds of such investment aimed at providing funding for each individual. The government investment was later increased to £180,000, and the American Ireland Fund also helped by underwriting six extra Bursaries a year. This Fund was started some time ago by Dr Tony O'Reilly, Chairman and Chief Executive of Heinz Inc., and he and his associates have raised a great deal of money from Irish-American sources in the United States to help peace, reconciliation and reconstruction in Ireland.

The four original projects were all exciting. They included a study of the Navajo and Hopi Indians on a reservation in Arizona; an observation of the French-speaking and English-Speaking Canadians in Quebec, who have problems not unlike those of our own; a study of Northern Ireland expatriates in Boston, incorporating work at the Robert F. Kennedy Centre for Human Rights; and living and working in an orphanage in Mexico. The reactions of the participants were equally exciting, as recorded in their evaluation reports.

*

"I have to say that my hosts were the finest people that I have ever come across and they treated me like their own son for the three weeks."

"The children at the orphanage were a miracle in their own right; they taught me more about life in one week than I ever dreamed of learning."

"I found I fulfilled many of my personal objectives whilst being able to look at the problems of politics in Northern Ireland and compare them to life problems for everyday survival in Mexico."

"This was the opportunity of a lifetime, a chance in a lifetime. The whole experience in Mexico opened my eyes to the real world; it made me appreciate everything I've got, thankful for the love I have always been shown by the family, but most of all I think the Spirit of Enniskillen showed me that the people of Northern Ireland are fighting over nothing. We are so insular and narrow-minded that we can't see that we have no justice for war, no cause for fighting and definitely no right to judge who have the right to live."

"I had feared that once back in an enclosed society all my lessons learnt in Arizona would fade. However, I find they became predominant in my mind."

"In a sense the end of our travelling was merely the beginning."

"We accepted each other as we were and as a result eight more people in our society are united in friendship with a strong desire for the troubles in our land to cease."

*

These kind of reactions made a deep impression on me and on my seven other colleagues on the selection panel, which is chaired by Gerry Burns, who had done such good work with the Enniskillen Appeal Fund. There were a large number of applicants the first year, but we anticipate a much greater interest in subsequent years. We are looking for the kind of young people who might benefit most from such a Bursary and who will have the right qualities to be good ambassadors for Northern Ireland. And, most important, we try to select the type of young person who is prepared to bring something back to his or her community. Some of the applications are most moving. One young man from a troubled area in Belfast wrote with a cry from the heart. He said that he had been born and reared in the Troubles and knew nothing else. All his friends and family had been affected, and he knew nothing about life apart from what he had experienced in his own restricted area. He was pleading,

"There's got to be something better outside of this place, and please will you allow me to see it".

Personally it is an honour to be a member of the selection panel and it has been my great pleasure to meet the participants because it gives me hope for the future as I listen to them expressing their hopes. I am confident that the Enniskillen Bursaries will continue to attract support and that they will continue to make an impact. Two Bursaries are reserved for Fermanagh participants each year, and I know that this causes a "stir" among local young people even if they are not successful, it's something that is talked about. The "Spirit of Enniskillen" Bursaries are like a beacon in that they are giving such an opportunity to the young. My generation failed to bring peace to our land, and I have a feeling that our young people will handle it better than we did. Perhaps it's not for me to speculate, but I have little doubt that the "Spirit of Enniskillen" Bursaries were a direct result of the bomb and of our response to it. Dr Mawhinney set it in motion, and who knows what seeds for good will be sown by the young people in years to come. It is very much an example of something really positive – arising out of the carnage of Enniskillen.

There were other developments also worth mentioning. The Rotary Clubs of Great Britain and Ireland raised nearly £20,000 and this was donated to the Erne Hospital to help furnish two rooms – one for the relatives of patients, and one for the hospital chaplains who, until recently, had to organize their business in someone else's office or even in the corridors. The chaplains do a great deal of good work, and I know from experience how they help to foster better relationships. When I was in the Erne Hospital with loss of memory I was asked to share in a communion service by the local rector, Canon McCarthy, who was attending a parishioner, and I greatly appreciated the offer. The hospital is one of those areas where we have a truly united community. When you are ill it does not matter whether the nurse or the doctor is a Roman Catholic or a Protestant, or neither.

The reaction to the Enniskillen bomb took many forms, including the formation of a local group called Enniskillen

Together. This was largely the brain-child of John Maxwell, whose son Paul was killed several years earlier in the IRA explosion which also killed Lord Mountbatten of Burma and members of his family. They died when their fishing boat was blown up, off the coast at Mullaghmore in County Sligo.

The Enniskillen Together movement works for outreach in areas where there is a need for bridge-building and they are doing great work. One of their projects which has made local headlines is the establishment of an integrated school, where Protestant and Roman Catholic children are educated together. People outside Northern Ireland may not be aware that the education system in the Province is organized largely on religious lines, and that many of our children do not meet their Protestant or Roman Catholic counterparts until they leave school. There is something to be said for a system of integrated education which brings the children together sooner rather than later. However, there are few developments in Ulster which are straightforward or uncomplicated. Some people would say that integrated education has its drawbacks. They argue that there is little point in a system which takes the children of moderate parents away from the classrooms of the largely one-religion schools who then miss this leavening influence. Others argue that there is already a certain degree of integration taking place in these schools which cater largely for one or other of the communities. However, I support the idea of integrated education because it seems worth promoting, in so far as it allows young people from each community to learn about each other at an earlier stage. Most important, they have an opportunity to learn about the things which they have in common, and not just those which can divide them.

In this context I am keen to support any worthwhile project which can lead to greater community understanding. One of the more encouraging developments took place some three weeks after the bomb when nearly five hundred schoolteachers from Fermanagh, Protestants and Roman Catholics, met in Enniskillen to discuss areas of mutual understanding and to try to work out ways in which young people could be encouraged to work together for tolerance and reconciliation.

This is not the kind of thing that can be fostered overnight. One of the problems of Northern Ireland is its long legacy of mistrust and misunderstanding, and this cannot be explained away in one or two meetings. But it is encouraging to know that so many of our teachers and educationalists can come together to address these issues and to think of ways in which a more positive and mutually understanding attitude can be fostered. One of the most notable developments has been the closer relationship between two of our leading Grammar Schools, St Michael's, which is mainly Roman Catholic, and Portora Royal School, which is mainly Protestant. The pupils share in various activities, including sport, and this is good for the future. There is perhaps a danger in trying to force the pace too quickly or in making too fulsome claims for bridge-building, but there is no doubt that quiet, sustained efforts at togetherness are bound to pay dividends in the future. This is true not only of Enniskillen but of Northern Ireland as a whole. I believe that nearly four thousand young people in the Belfast area took part in a service at St Anne's Cathedral just after the bombing, and this helped to establish a cross-community campaign with the theme "Choose Life". The idea was to maintain the momentum for a year, and there are hopes that there will be a lasting affect by establishing closer co-operation among the Youth Departments of the churches. All of these projects and movements and stirrings arose from, or reflect, the "Spirit of Enniskillen".

People ask me, "What do you really think of Enniskillen now? Are things better than they were?" This is a difficult question to answer. If someone came back to the town after a long absence, he or she might not notice any great physical difference. But I believe that there is a difference. There's a feeling of hope, and, to a strange degree, a greater hope than before. A lot of hearts were softened and a great many attitudes were changed. This is something which would be difficult to measure in concrete terms. Fermanagh folk are not the kind who put on great displays of togetherness to impress people, but that feeling is there. We have all come a long way in the past twenty or thirty years, and there's much more mixing of the two communities than when I first came to the town. It is worth remembering that this togetherness was taking place slowly, even before the bomb. But it is also true that differences still exist. People still hold to their own ways of worshipping and of looking at things, but there is a degree of blurring around the hard edges. The bomb seemed to give all of this an impetus. It literally ripped a hole in the heart of the community, but miraculously that heart-beat continues and grows steadily stronger. There's a great local pride in Enniskillen and also an awareness that we have much to share. I don't think Enniskillen will ever forget the bomb, but somehow it has made all of us realize that the old ways were not necessarily the best ways and that we have to keep working and hoping and co-operating for a better future.

When the Bursaries scheme was being launched I was asked to make a speech, and I used the opportunity to define what I think is the "Spirit of Enniskillen". "It is a spirit of love where there might have been hatred, of tolerance where there might have been retribution, and of reconciliation where there might have been division." I said it then, and I believe it now. With God's help, the "Spirit of Enniskillen" will point the way to a better future for everyone. Love can, and will, triumph over hatred.

CHAPTER TWELVE

The Bottom Line

One of the most shocking things I ever had said to me came from Neil Kinnock, the leader of the Labour Party. I use the term "shocking" not in the usual way of meaning "alarming" or "sensational", but as something that literally shook me to the core. We were talking in his office at the House of Commons, where I was making in a visit, and he asked me, "How are you coping with all the pressures and the publicity?" I replied, "As best I can, but it isn't easy. We are still looking for privacy, and somewhere to get away from it all." Then I asked him a question, "Can you tell me how I can go back to being the Gordon Wilson I like to think I was, the day before the bomb? Can I go back to being 'the wee draper in the wee town?'" Neil Kinnock paused for a moment and looked me straight in the eye. It was not just his words but also the way that he said them which shook me rigid. He replied slowly, "You never will get back to being the Gordon Wilson you were." I looked at him and realized he was absolutely right. It was as if someone had suddenly opened a window on the future and I saw what, possibly, I had known already deep in my subconscious but which, perhaps, I did not want to admit to. But the longer I live, the surer I am that Neil Kinnock spoke the truth. I can never go back. The bomb has changed everything, and perhaps if I learn that alone I may be able to cope a little more realistically with whatever lies in store.

Things are different, in so many ways. It's a fact of life, and we have to learn to accept it. There's an empty chair in our home, and we have to go on from that reality. It is different, and it will go on being different. I pray that I will get the strength to cope for a long or a short time, whatever it is to be. If I was asked, "Would you prefer that it all had never happened?", I would say, "Of course", but that's outside my control. I have no choice, nor have any of the others. We have to get on with it.

Physically I'm not the man I was. I have a numbness in my arm which, the doctors tell me, is a form of arthritis, and I find it tiring. I used to be able to do a full day's work, and carry on into the evening. Now I've had enough by lunchtime, and I need to lie down. My concentration is not as good as it used to be, and, some time ago, I began to lose my keen interest in my business. I have been a draper all my life, and I have enjoyed the challenge of trading, of buying and selling, of being a part of the business community. There's a great deal you can learn about human nature, when you run a draper's shop! Some years ago, I managed to buy a large consignment of good quality suits from an Ulster manufacturer, at a very good price, and I offered them as a bargain in my shop. I went even further and offered the suits in pairs at a really keen price. However, I soon began to notice that the professional men in town and their wives, who might have been expected to snap up such a bargain, in most cases bought one suit and fussed over it, but not two. Then one day just before closing time a lorry stopped outside the shop and two roughly-dressed men jumped out. They had seen the advertisement for these "Bargain" suits in the local papers, and they came into the shop. Within minutes they had picked out two suits each, paid for them with fistfuls of notes, and left the shop! On my way home I thought again of the old adage, "Never judge a book by its cover!" Seriously, however, I enjoyed my life as draper and the cut and thrust of business life. But after the bomb it just didn't seem to matter as much any more.

Sometimes people tend to overlook that I was caught up in the actual bomb itself, apart from the heart-break and trauma afterwards. I'm not trying to make a special plea for myself or to dwell on my injuries, but if you've been blasted to the ground and showered with falling masonry, it's bound to have an effect on your body as well as your mind. There is a sense still of physical limitation, and my debility shows itself in all sorts of ways. Things I once would have taken in my stride now tire me physically or mentally, or both. The other day I was totally exhausted after cutting the lawn. There's no doubt that you slow down as you get older, but the injuries of the bomb have contributed to my slowing-down. I still find it difficult to sleep without tablets, and yet I tried to do without them. Sometimes when I'm tired during the day I get a bit snappy, and certainly a bit more snappy than the real Gordon Wilson would like himself to be, and I tend to suffer fools less gladly. But maybe that shows that Gordon Wilson is human after all. I don't like people putting me on a pedestal. Most days, however, I try to keep myself perked up, and I greatly enjoy making conversation with my old friends over a cup of coffee. Yet there are still days when I'm not on top form, and the conversation seems irrelevant. Maybe we all have those days, and we all have to learn how to cope with them.

However, I am aware also of the great blessings in my life and of the many things for which I ought to be, can be, and am, thankful. And at the top of that list is my wife and family. There are no words in my vocabulary to express what I owe to Joan. She is my wife, partner, friend, the one who "puts up with me", and also the mother of my children. You can't get any closer than that. She opened up a whole new dimension to me, in a way that only someone close can do this sort of thing. And she surprised me by what she said. She was talking about my survival.

"I'm so glad that you were spared, for we could always depend on you. Marie always admired that quality of yours, going right down the middle, always trying to say and to do the right thing. Even when I joked to her about you she would get cross and say, 'How dare you say that about my Dad!'

"I think that the bomb has brought us even closer, and we need each other more day by day. I don't think that I could have said what you said on television. At that stage I would not have been able to find those words about not bearing a grudge, but I grew into that, quietly and slowly. I do not bear a grudge. But I still have the questions: 'How could they do it?' and 'How can they face their maker?'

"When people ask me what is Gordon really like, the answer is simple. 'The Gordon Wilson you saw on television is the Gordon Wilson I know. He is as straight as a die, and he always will be.'"

Such talk is beyond me. It's difficult to accept yourself as someone else sees you, even someone very close like your wife. I honestly feel that what I said and did was not, as I would say, "a big deal". I was simply given the grace and strength to do as I did, and I would hope that I would do the same all over again if the testing came. But I am also aware of the effect that all of this has had on my family, who have been largely in the background. Peter has been quietly supportive, and I realize that he has had to deal with remarks from others who were critical of what I have or have not done, and for seeming to favour one side or the other. Peter has been a great, steadying influence not only in helping on the business side where he managed part of the shop, but in giving me strong moral support while I have had to make many of my responses under the glare of publicity. So, too, has Julie Anne. I know that she dislikes intensely all the massive publicity, and that she really wanted to be left in private with us to do our grieving. And yet she understood why this could not be so. I know that she misses Marie deeply, and that as a result of the bomb she has been able to take a long, hard look at life and to work out the things that are really important.

For my part these are the big things, like having a close-knit family, and the little things, like still being able to drive a car, to read, to meet my friends, and to play a round of golf. When I was younger I used to take many things far too seriously. I was extremely keen on indoor bowls, and I played bowls for Ireland five times over two seasons, in Home International tournaments. It became almost like a religion, it was so ingrained. I used to go around the countryside to bowl, even when I would have been better spending more time with my family. But then one day I was beaten in the first round of a local tournament by an unknown who was just starting off. After that, I gave up completely. I just simply walked away, because I could not bear the thought of slipping down the ratings and of being beaten by people whom I could have disposed of easily, in my prime. It proved that my technique had fallen apart, and it was time to quit. That seems to be an awful, conceited attitude, but I was the kind of man who could not take on bowls, or anything else, without being serious.

Now I have a different attitude entirely. The surface details of life are not so important, but it's the hidden qualities like caring, and tolerance and patience, and concern for others, that matter. It no longer seems to be the end of the world if I happen to miss an edition of "Panorama" or "News at Ten"! The little things have been pushed into their own perspective. Sometimes I listen wistfully to other parents who, unwittingly, talk about the "problems" of dealing with their teenage children, to do with their schooling or the cost of their keep or of staying out late at night; and I say to myself, "I wish we had that problem with Marie". Some people don't realize how lonely you can feel in such a conversation.

On the other hand, there have been many moments of re-assurance and of continuing comfort – including all the lovely things which were said and done, and the fine sentiments which were expressed as a result of what happened in Enniskillen. One of my most treasured possessions, which I keep in my wallet, came from a clergyman who wrote, "God be with you. May you hear His 'I love you' through the pain of your sadness, and may Marie be yours for ever in the Resurrections of Jesus. Thank you for what you have said and done." His letter was all the more treasured because he himself bore the scars of trying to build bridges in his community.

Roughly a year after the bomb went off, I listened to three local clergymen on the BBC "Thought for the Day", and they provided some deep insights into what Enniskillen had meant to them and the community, and how we all had grown through that awful experience. Dean John McCarthy, who ministered to me in the Erne Hospital shortly after the bomb, spoke on radio about the centenary of the birth of T.S. Eliot. He said,

Many of his great poems were written in the early Forties in wartime London, when, surrounded by carnage and destruction, this profoundly Christian poet was moved to explore the great themes of redemption and forgiveness in this unlikely setting. Because of the background of his work, Eliot has, I think, a great deal to say to us today. . . .

The marked foundations of a disfigured building in the centre of the town of Enniskillen are still to be seen today. One hardly needs a reminder of that totally unnecessary devastation which hit the town twelve months ago, and yet from these marred foundations a message of hope and forgiveness reached out into the world around. It appeared to many that a great day was coming for the people of our Province as new relationships were cemented and people dared to dream unimaginable dreams. Perhaps it didn't quite work out in the way we had hoped but words were spoken which moved millions, and in this respect things could never be the same again. It became for many an opportunity to see new possibilities, to make a fresh start and to have high hopes that tomorrow would dawn bright and fresh and fair. Every day is and must continue to be an opportunity for a new beginning. Eliot reaches the end of his search for God and finds it only a beginning. "In my end is my beginning' and finding that reality always leads to hope even in the midst of death and despair. "So the darkness shall be the light and the stillness the dancing."

"And all shall be well and all manner of things shall be well."

The Reverend David Cupples, the Minister of the Presbyterian Church in Enniskillen, had gone through the harrowing experience of losing six of his congregation in the bomb, and of trying to bring comfort to the injured and to the bereaved. And yet he was able to say these words, a year later, in his "Thought for the Day" broadcast.

Today is 8th November – the date last year of the Enniskillen bombing. In our town today there will be tension and anxiety. Many people will feel their stomach tighten and wonder how to face the day. How will they spend it? What will they say to people? How will they handle their emotions and memories of one year ago? I am thinking especially of the bereaved and injured, but I am sure there will not be a single person in the town who will not be affected in some way today, and on Sunday too. I will be busy today. There are two services in our church – one this morning for relatives of the victims, and a special time of prayer tonight for our province. But I too will pause and reflect. What did it all mean? Where are we now? I can't answer the great question of what change it has made in our community. There is nothing obvious to point to, yet in the long term it might still prove to have been a moment when peace came a step closer. I can, however, tell you some of my more personal thoughts today.

I will think of the place for tears in our experience. Jesus wept. He allows the broken-hearted to weep. His promises were given to wipe tears away, not to make them unnecessary. Then he looks to his people for tears of repentance, tears of compassion for our society. Some may think trust in God means smiles all the way. I think God is wondering where are those who will weep as Jesus wept over Jerusalem.

I will think too of the choices that we face today. It is time to realize that spiritual and moral choices are more fundamental than political ones. If we seek first the kingdom of God and his righteousness will not peace be added unto us also? The deepest division in Ireland is not the border. It is the division between people and between man and God. The reconciliation God gives happens at the foot of Christ's cross where our sins are forgiven and we are made new by His Spirit, empowered to love our neighbour and even our enemy. Personally and as a community we need a spiritual awakening.

Finally I can look back on a hard year and say God is to be praised. I know what Paul means when he says "sorrowful yet always rejoicing". There are tears of joy as we receive Christ's comfort in sorrow, experience his presence in the crisis, and witness his power to change lives.

May I thank all of you who have prayed for the people of Enniskillen before, and will pray for us today. Let us who know the Lord, face this day remembering he is still in control, and remembering his words, "Men ought always to pray and not give up".

Monsignor Sean Cahill, the Parish Priest in Enniskillen, was one of the first people to comfort me in the Erne Hospital on that dreadful morning of the bomb. A year later on radio I listened to the inspiring words of a man who touched on very deep themes when he talked about our town, and all that had happened. He said:

When I think of Enniskillen, I think of a beautiful island town, steeped in history, its one long street meandering from the east to the west bridge, lapped on all sides by the clear waters of Lough Erne.

I think too of a proud people with a sense of history, a practical people with a sense of humour, a neighbourly people with a slight wariness of the newcomer – not born between the bridges.

When I think of Enniskillen, I remember the horror of a November day, the shattered building, the crushed bodies, the choking dust, the heart-rending tears of so many families. I remember the crippling fear, the cries of shame, the awful silence and then the words of forgiveness, the reconciling hands.

During the year I came across the prayer of an unknown Jewish woman, found on a piece of wrapping paper in Ravensbruck concentration camp. It went like this:

O Lord, remember not only the men and women of goodwill but also those of illwill. But do not remember the suffering they have inflicted upon us; remember the fruits we bore, thanks to this suffering: our comradeship, our loyalty, our humility, the courage, the generosity, the greatness of heart which has grown out of this; and when they come to judgement, let all the fruits that we have borne be their forgiveness.

This woman, a victim too of inhumanity, learned in the cauldron of suffering the power and inspiration of forgiveness. I said to myself – This is humanity at its best. This is the Gospel truly alive. This is real holiness. And then. . . . I found myself remembering Enniskillen. . . .

To my mind there is something profound and beautiful in the words of these men, who represent the different traditions in Enniskillen. Of course there were some harsh words from others, and no doubt there are still bruised emotions beneath the surface, but I believe that the Enniskillen bomb brought out the best in people even though it had been planted with the worst of motives. I am certain, however, that long after Gordon Wilson and the other survivors have gone, and even after the names of the victims are but a distant memory, the Remembrance Day bombing in Enniskillen will not be forgotten. The very fact of the killing and maiming of innocent people gathered round a

Cenotaph will be recalled by people everywhere as an intrusion upon sacred ground where all mankind pauses to honour those who died in war.

The seriousness of all of this never leaves me, but, thank God, I hope that I have been able to retain my sense of perspective and my humour. It's important to have the kind of family who will keep your feet on the ground, and my family appreciated my story of a young policeman on duty in Enniskillen who put me in my place and got his priorities right! I had been in a local travel agent's shop booking a holiday. There had been some difficulty, but when the travel assistant phoned London to provide our names, the girl at the other end said, "Is that the Gordon Wilson I saw on television the other night?" I have to confess, God forgive me, that I came out of the shop feeling about ten feet tall! However, I was in for a rude awakening; when I left the shop I saw a young policeman standing beside my car with a determined look on his face.

He had that air of studied politeness which policemen and traffic wardens use when they know that they have a strong case, and you have not! "Do you realize, Sir," he asked, "That half of your car is parked on the double-yellow line?" I sized him up before replying, "I do Constable, but do you realize that half the car is not parked on the double-yellow line?" There was a trace of a smile on his lips, and thankfully he had a sense of humour. He said, "I've half a mind to book you for illegal parking, but I'll let you off this time." Away he went, and there was me thinking that I had been a "big man" known to everyone in the United Kingdom, and a young policeman in my own town didn't even know me from Adam! That sort of thing is just what you need for the ego.

Another amusing story, which occurred around the same time, had an unconsciously deeper twist. One day I was walking across a carpark in Belfast, after appearing on a national television programme, and a little old lady ran across a stretch of wasteland to greet me. She shook my hand warmly and said, "Thank God for all that you've done, Gordon Wilson. You're the only politician we've got"! That really made me smile, because a political career, or even politics, is the last thing on my mind. But, unknowingly, she struck a deeper chord which made me think about the path I ought to follow.

After the bomb, and all the publicity, some people believed that I might have used the opportunity to start a peace organization of one kind or another. That is something which I have steadily resisted, because I have always felt that this has not been my role. The *Belfast Telegraph* put the point well in an editorial published on 21st December 1987, just a few weeks after the bombing.

What made Gordon Wilson such an unusually effective communicator, after the Enniskillen bombing, was his very ordinariness. Here was a simple, God-fearing man whose life had been touched by a great personal tragedy, and yet who bore "no ill will, no grudge'. He must have seemed a natural candidate to launch a new peace movement, but, as he revealed at the weekend, he declined to take up the offer. He had made his contribution, by talking movingly about the dying minutes of his daughter and touching the hearts of millions. The rest was for other people, with other gifts.

His decision to stay in Enniskillen, rather than embark on a speaking tour, was further evidence of his innate good sense. Others before him, in the Peace People, chose the other road, from the best of motives, but found that in the end peace is a job for politicians. No matter how many thousands can be persuaded to march for peace, or to honour the peacemakers, they themselves cannot bring the miracle about. Peace will be built on sound politics, as well as a change of heart, and while a peace movement can bring pressure to bear on the politicians, it can also raise false hopes.

The spirit of Gordon Wilson must live on into 1988, but it is the spirit of ordinary people, rather than exalted figureheads, getting on with their lives and refusing to be embittered by violence done to them. The message to anyone tempted into retaliation, by violence intended to be provocative, is to turn the other cheek if they can, and certainly not to seek revenge.

I have never wanted to create a peace movement as such. That is not my style. Of course I have asked myself, then and since, "What can I do?" Sometimes I have not slept too well, thinking about it. I ask myself, "Could I have done more, and if so, what should I have done?" I am realistic enough, and I have been sufficiently humbled by life, to allow myself to wait and to seek guidance. It may be that I have already done all that has been required of me at a particular time, and that by just being myself I have been able in an imperfect way to do my bit. But I know that if the way is to open up further for me, it will do so. Other people took several years to come to terms with what had happened to them and to find a way forward.

If you're asking me for a solution, you are asking the wrong man. Beware of the person who comes forward bearing a simple "solution" to our problems. I would not even begin to attempt any outline of a political settlement. That's for people who are more learned and more skilled in politics than I am. We are entering here into a complex area concerning the roots of Irish history, of people's rights to stay and to live in their country, and we're talking about different loyalties and aspirations, and remembering a terrible history, with all its bloodshed. Perhaps the biggest legacy of the present Troubles is those of us who have to pick up the pieces, the thousands of bereaved families and the tens of thousands of the injured and their relatives. That's a terrible legacy of suffering in any community, and only those who have been through the fire can really know what it's like. People in Northern Ireland who are not directly involved, like those in the United Kingdom and the Irish Republic, really do sympathize, but they can't understand it because they haven't been through it. The violence is a devastating condemnation of our whole society, and of both communities.

Since the present Troubles began there have been millions of words spoken by politicians, sociologists, commentators, reporters, and all kinds of experts, but words alone have not brought a solution. I am convinced, above all, that there will be no glimmer of a solution until the killing, all the killing, stops. The greater the killing, the greater the legacy of bitterness and hurt, and the harder it will be for people to start talking. The more killings there are, the worse it gets, and the harder it will be to find an answer. And yet there has to be an answer. Surely the minds and hearts of men and women can find a solution to what is in our terms a terrible and continuing problem, but which in the face of the momentous changes in Eastern Europe and Russia and other parts of the world, is only a chronic local difficulty? Who would have thought not so long ago that walls and barriers would have come tumbling down across Europe? Why can't this happen in Northern Ireland? I am sure that the majority of the people in Ireland want and indeed long for peace, and I am convinced that some day peace will come, but don't ask me how, and don't press me for a political blueprint. I just know in my heart that peace will come, and that we must go on striving to find it. Our Lord said, "Thou shalt love the Lord thy God with all thy heart, and with all thy soul, and with all thy mind. This is the first and great commandment. And the second is like unto it, Thou shalt love thy neighbour as thyself." It's as difficult and as all-powerful as that. Maybe we are so familiar with the words that only a tragedy as great as Enniskillen can shake us to our roots with the awfulness of what can happen if, individually and collectively, we cease to love our neighbour as ourselves.

One of the most memorable moments of my life occurred in Enniskillen Methodist Church one evening when the Chairman of the World Methodist Council, Bishop Lawi Imathui from Kenya, presented me with the medal and ribbon of the 1988 World Methodist Peace Award. It was quite a daunting occasion, and I was required to say a few words. I made the point that, as I listened to the other speakers, I became more nervous, embarrassed and unworthy, and I said, "I am nervous because I knew that I had to stand up and talk, after all that had been said in my church and among my friends who know the real Gordon Wilson. I am embarrassed because I kept asking myself, 'What's all the fuss about?' I feel bemused. The half of what has been said cannot be true, but only you can decide which half is not! I feel unworthy when I look at the men and women who were previous recipients of the Award. Either I am stepping out of my depth, or else my friends are going to have to pay a lot more respect to Gordon Wilson!" Seriously, however, I made several observations about the nature of peace, and these words still apply today:

This is a Peace Award. "What peace?" you may well ask. Indeed you might well ask that poor woman who lost her daughter as well as her father in an explosion in Benburb only last week. In that sense of the word, there *is* no Peace, certainly not yet. But Peace will come, maybe not tomorrow but come it will, because Good must triumph over Evil, and Love will triumph over Hatred.

But my Peace is of another kind. Perhaps it is really the same Peace, in the end, or indeed a better one. I enjoy the Peace of knowing beyond doubt that Marie is in the presence of her Lord, and that, with God's will, we shall again hold her hand. I enjoy the Peace of knowing that God is good, and my prayer is that he will be merciful to me, a sinner. I enjoy the Peace of knowing that God is love, and that his grace is sufficient. I enjoy the fact that others have found Peace. A letter in the past week, from a man known to two people in this company, said, and I quote, "I feel impelled to let you know that it was the terrible tragedy of Enniskillen in November 1987, which started me on the road to closer union with the Lord". The deaths of eleven gentle people in Enniskillen and more than two and a half thousand in Northern Ireland will become worthwhile when enough people are moved in that way. I have said all that I can or want to say tonight. May I finish with the words of John Greenleaf Whittier, the New England poet and hymn writer, who says it all infinitely better than I could ever hope to do:

Follow with reverent steps the great example
of him whose holy work was doing good;
so shall the wide earth seem our Father's temple,
each loving life a psalm of gratitude.

Then shall all shackles fall; the stormy clangour of wild
war-music o'er the earth shall cease;
Love shall tread out the baleful fire of anger,
And in its ashes, plant the tree of peace.

*

We have come a long way on our journey. The tragedy of Enniskillen is not a road which I would have chosen. If I had known in advance I would have pleaded like our Lord in Gethsemane, "Father if it be possible, let this cup pass from me; nevertheless not as I will, but as Thou wilt." And I am sure that all of us, and all who have been touched by the tragedy of

Northern Ireland, would want to speak likewise. But we cannot change what's happened. We have to go on living, as best we can, with whatever strength we are given to do so. If I have a message, it is this – I believe very strongly in the words of our Lord when he said, "A new commandment I give you, That ye love one another." That's basically it. Those words about love were burned into me by Marie's experience. Her last words were "Daddy, I love you very much". She went out on words of love, and I have to stay on that plane. Hopefully and thankfully, with God's Grace, I will keep on trying to do that.

The first and last words in this whole story are about love. That's what helps me to keep going, to get through my days and to sleep at nights. Love God and your neighbour. In life and after death there's only one ultimate standard by which we are judged. Marie showed that, to us all, as she lay under the rubble at the Cenotaph holding my hand, with her life slipping away. The bottom line is love. There's nothing more I can say.